SORTING OUT ETHICS

SORTING OUT ETHICS

BY

R. M. HARE

CLARENDON PRESS · OXFORD
1997

Oxford University Press, Great Clarendon Street, Oxford OX2 6DP

Oxford New York
Athens Auckland Bangkok Bogota Bombay
Buenos Aires Calcutta Cape Town Dar es Salaam
Delhi Florence Hong Kong Istanbul Karachi
Kuala Lumpur Madras Madrid Melbourne
Mexico City Nairobi Paris Singapore
Taipei Tokyo Toronto Warsaw

and associated companies in
Berlin Ibadan

Oxford is a trade mark of Oxford University Press

Published in the United States by
Oxford University Press Inc., New York

British Library Cataloguing in Publication Data
Data available

Library of Congress Cataloging in Publication Data
Hare, R. M. (Richard Mervyn)
Sorting out ethics / R. M. Hare
Includes bibliographical references and index.
1. Ethics I. Title.
BJ1012.H31352 1997 170—dc21 97–8001
ISBN 0–19–823727–8

1 3 5 7 9 10 8 6 4 2

Typeset by Invisible Ink
Printed in Great Britain
on acid-free paper by
Biddles Ltd, Guildford and King's Lynn

PREFACE

The core of this book is my Axel Hägerström Lectures, given in Uppsala in 1991. I had planned to incorporate these, together with revisions of other papers, into a full-length book giving my considered views on ethical theory. It was to have been given as the José Ferrater Mora Lectures at Girona in Catalonia. But this too ambitious project was defeated by a series of strokes, which rendered me incapable, not only of typing with more than one hand, but of thinking book-length thoughts. I was very sorry to have to cancel my visit to Catalonia, to which I had been looking forward with pleasure.

Formerly, when writing a book, I used to hold the whole of it in my head from start to finish. This is the only way to avoid repetitions and even contradictions. But I can no longer do it. So I have had to compromise, with the helpful advice of the Oxford University Press, and publish the lectures with three major additions. The first of these is an attempt to justify the whole enterprise of applying philosophy of language to ethics. It is a revised version of my contribution to the De Gruyter *Handbuch Sprachphilosophie*, and gives a conspectus of my entire thinking. The second is an introduction to my lecture course in Oxford and Florida, omitted from the five lectures given in Uppsala because of lack of time.

The Axel Hägerström Lectures follow. They were delivered originally under the title, 'A Taxonomy of Ethical Theories'. The first and second of these were mostly new; the rest had many sources. They are partly a distillation of lectures given over the years in Oxford, Florida, and elsewhere, much revised, condensed, and, I hope, improved. My practice has been to give lectures shaped round a nucleus which remained basically the same, to which I added other lectures from time to time. Many of these additions were intended to illustrate the uses of ethical theory by applying it to practical problems. They have mostly been collected into volumes and published already. I hope that one other such volume will appear. But the nucleus, giving my latest considered thoughts, could not be published while I was still lecturing. This formed the main part of the Axel Hägerström Lectures. I have to thank the very intelligent audience at Uppsala for giving them such a stimulating reception. I am printing them as delivered, with a few afterthoughts, but retaining the style of an oral presentation.

Last, I have reprinted my paper 'Could Kant have been a Utilitarian?' from *Utilitas* 5, which has also appeared in *Kant and Critique*, edited by R. M. Dancy. It was given, among other occasions, in Stockholm on the same visit to Sweden. I owe so many of my own ideas to Kant, and my interpretation of him as a quasi-utilitarian is so unorthodox (though it now has supporters), that I thought it worth reprinting here.

It will be obvious that a book so structured is bound to contain overlaps. For example, points are mentioned briefly in Chapter 1 but taken up in more detail in Chapters 3 to 7; and my interpretation of Kant figures in many of the earlier chapters before being fully explored in Chapter 8. This is unavoidable if the chapters are to be read independently. Some people may want to read just Chapter 1 as a summary of my ideas; but others may find this too difficult and skip on to Chapter 2, which is much easier. And some may not be interested in questions of Kantian exegesis. For these reasons I have decided to put up with some overlaps; but these are clearly signposted.

I have to thank others besides the Swedes for comments on various versions of these lectures. They are too many to list; but I have given the names of those whose writings I found of most help with the Kant chapter in the bibliography. This has been expanded into a full list of my philosophical writings, as an aid to those who wish to study my ideas, with the addition of abstracts of my more important recent papers. I owe a lot to the excellent bibliography compiled by Ulla Wessels for the two volumes of *Zum moralischen Denken* (H 1995*a*), the proceedings of a conference on my work.

I have used an author–date system of reference, because it avoids footnotes; but I have not thought it necessary to cite the page numbers in cases where it is easy to find the passage referred to. The reason is that many of the articles have appeared in several places with different paginations; and the same applies to the numerous translations of my works. In the case of references to older writers who are published in many editions it has usually been best to cite the section or chapter, or, in the case of Plato, Aristotle, and Kant, the pages of the standard editions.

I offer this taxonomy of ethical theories to all those who are lost in the moral maze, including many of my philosophical colleagues. They are lost because, like most of those who hold forth on moral questions in the media, they have no map of the maze. This it has been my aim to provide.

CONTENTS

PART I

THE ENTERPRISE OF MORAL PHILOSOPHY

I

PHILOSOPHY OF LANGUAGE IN ETHICS

1.1. ETHICS, or moral philosophy, is the point at which philosophers come closest to practical issues in morals and politics. It thus provides a major part of the practical justification for doing philosophy (H 1971c: 98). If, therefore, philosophy of language can be shown to have a crucial contribution to make to ethics, this greatly increases the practical relevance of the discipline. But it is very important to be clear about what the contribution is.

The following programme looks promising at first sight. Philosophy of language is concerned above all with the study of the concept of *meaning* in the various senses of that word. But the meanings of moral words and sentences, in at least some senses, determine the logic of inferences in which they appear. So a study of the meanings of moral words or sentences, or of what people mean when they utter them, ought to enable us to investigate the logical properties of what they say, and thus decide whether what they say is self-consistent, what it implies, and in general which arguments (in the sense of reasonings) are good ones and which are not. So philosophy of language, applied to moral language, ought to be able to provide a logical structure for our moral thinking. And since our moral thinking often founders for lack of such a structure, that would be no small gain.

Revised from H 1996a.

There are a great many pitfalls to be avoided in carrying out this programme; but I shall argue that it is in principle a feasible one. So let us first consider some possible objections to it. I shall be in danger of being misunderstood if I do not make clear at the start that philosophy of language is not the same as linguistic philosophy. The former is a branch of philosophy, co-ordinate with philosophy of science, philosophy of law, philosophy of history, etc. To say that a philosopher is doing philosophy of language does not presuppose that he is doing it by any particular method, or in accordance with the tenets of any particular school. Philosophers of language can be realists or the opposite, intuitionists or the opposite, and so on. If anybody were to say, like Plato on some interpretations, that words have meaning because they *stand for* eternally existing non-sensible entities up in Heaven, he would still be doing philosophy of language, but would obviously not be a linguistic philosopher. But see H 1982a, esp. ch. 4, for a more 'linguistic' interpretation of Plato.

A linguistic philosopher is someone who believes in a particular way of doing philosophy (*any* kind of philosophy, not just philosophy of language), namely that which consists in studying the meanings of words that present philosophical problems, and so unravelling the problems. He will advocate, like Carnap (1932), an 'Überwindung der Metaphysik durch logische Analyse der Sprache'. To make my own position clear, I am a linguistic philosopher of a sort, but not of such an extreme sort as Carnap. I believe that metaphysics does not have to be overcome, nor even superseded; as inherited from Aristotle, it is a respectable and central branch of philosophy, and only certain bogus impersonations of it are suspect. Ever since Aristotle and before, it has used linguistic methods. A great many problems which are called 'ontological' are in fact to be resolved by careful attention to the words which give rise to them; and this is true above all in ethics. But I regard this, not as a way of overcoming metaphysics, but as a way of doing it competently—of mastering it, if we may so mistranslate 'überwinden'; and I believe that this way of doing it has yielded results when practised by all the great metaphysicians up to the present day. So I am not against metaphysics—only against some wholly spurious 'philosophical' and 'theological' activities which have in recent times usurped the name; they would be better called 'mephistics', because they are attempts, like that of Mephistopheles in *Faust*, to get philosophers to sell their souls for fantasies.

I wish to consider two possible objections to the programme I projected at the beginning. The first says, 'Facts about particular languages, including facts about how people use words in particular cultures, are contingent facts. They therefore cannot be used to establish necessary truths such as we are looking for in ethics. We do not want to be told how particular people or cultures use the moral words; we want to be shown what *is* right or wrong, and to be shown by secure reasoning that this is necessarily the case.'

The second objection is related to the first: it says, 'Moral reasoning has to be concerned with moral facts, which are facts not about words but about the world—facts about the existence of moral values in the world. The study of words could never yield such facts.' Answers to both these objections can be given. For the first, consider the position of ordinary logic. It would be a mistake to suppose that logic discovers only contingent truths about language; but it is also a mistake to think that logic is independent of the study of language. It is a necessary truth that, in one common meaning of 'all' and the other words used, if all the books on the top shelf are by Wittgenstein, and this is a book on the top shelf, then this is by Wittgenstein. But in order to establish that this is a necessary truth, we have to be assured that the words are being used and understood in the senses that make it so. Logic is, at least in part, the study of the words which people use in their discourse, to ascertain which of the things they say are, as they use the words, necessary truths.

This does not make the truths of logic contingent. It is of course a contingent fact that people do use certain sounds with certain senses. But to ask in what senses they use them is to ask according to what rules or conventions, logical and semantical, they use them. And it is not a contingent fact, but a tautology, that anyone who is using the words in those senses will be committing logical errors if he does not observe those rules. To take the same example: it is a contingent fact that someone is using 'all' in the sense that he is. But it is not a contingent fact that, if he is using it in *that* sense (namely the sense in which the above hypothetical is necessarily true), the hypothetical is necessarily true. What makes the sense *that* sense is that it is the sense which makes that hypothetical necessarily true.

1.2. Words, including words like 'all', have their meaning determined by the conventions according to which we use them. And the conventions are in part logical ones, which determine what implies what, what we can consistently say, etc. One is not being a conventionalist in any bad sense if one states the obvious truth that studying what the conventions are for the use of words like 'all' (i.e. what logical rules they are governed by, as people use them) is the basis of the discovery of these logical rules.

To this it may be objected that people do not *have* to use words in accordance with those rules. Humpty Dumpty was quite right (Carroll 1872: 196). 'All' *could* have meant the same as 'some' does now—which is to say that the rules which determine its meaning and the implications of propositions containing it might have been different, and like those which now determine the meaning and implications of 'some'. And Englishmen, Frenchmen, Germans, and Chinese use different sounds to express the same things. And the inventors of artificial languages like Carnap have a considerable liberty to invent new uses of words and symbols, and to invent, *pari passu* with this, new rules and conventions for their use. Here too, however, it has to be said that *if* a word is being used in any language (natural or artificial) to express the same meaning as a word in some other language, it is bound by the same logical rules. If it were bound by different rules, it would not express the same meaning. A word in Chinese is not the equivalent of 'all' unless, when used in the corresponding Chinese hypothetical about Wittgenstein, it makes it necessarily true.

So, if logic as a whole involves the study of words in this way, the same will be true of that branch of logic called theoretical ethics. I call theoretical ethics a branch of logic because its principal aim is the discovery of ways of determining what arguments about moral questions are good ones, or how to tell sound from unsound reasoning in this area. It is, in particular, a branch of modal logic. 'Ought', which we may take as the simplest example of a word used typically in moral discourse (a moral word, for short), expresses a deontic

modality, and this is shown by the fact that deontic logics can be systematized which are in all or nearly all respects analogous to the
other kinds of modal logic (Prior 1955: III. i. 6). The same is even more
clearly true of the word 'must': its use to express moral statements
like 'I must not tell her a lie' is analogous in most ways to its use to express alethic modal statements.

If, as is beginning to happen, viable systems of deontic logic can be
discovered which are adequate models of ordinary moral language,
they will do as much for the understanding of moral arguments as
ordinary logic does for the understanding of other arguments. So, although it is of course a contingent fact that English uses 'ought' to
express the meaning that it does, it is not contingent that *any* language that has an equivalent sentence—i.e. a way of expressing the
same thought—will be bound by the same rules of reasoning. And
what the rules are, as the word is normally used, is discovered by asking how it *is* normally used.

As before, we do not *have* to use it in that way. But when we are arguing about moral problems we are arguing about whether to accept
or reject certain moral judgements. Clearly, whether an argument is
a good argument for accepting or rejecting a certain judgement will
depend on what the judgement is. But *what* it is depends on what the
words used in expressing it are being understood to mean. If they
were being understood to mean something different, it would be a different judgement. But once we are committed to discussing whether
to accept or reject *that* judgement (i.e. the judgement which those
words express when they are taken in *that* way) we are committed to
following the rules of reasoning which that way of taking them determines. To take the words in that way is to accept that the judgement (with or without additional premisses) logically implies such
and such other judgements, is inconsistent with such and such other
judgements, and so on. So the sense of the words, as before, determines which arguments about the questions we are asking are sound
ones. Therefore, in order to determine whether they are sound, we
have to examine the senses of the words, i.e. the rules for their use in
arguments.

We can of course, as before, use words as we wish. But if we decide to use words differently from how we were using them when we posed our original problem, we shall no longer be posing the same problem. We are free to pose different problems; and that is what we shall be doing if the words mean something different. To revert to our original example: if what we had been asking had been, not whether all the books were by Wittgenstein, but whether some of them were, it would not have been a reason for answering 'No' that one of the books was not by Wittgenstein. So if, when we said 'all', we had been using the word in the same sense as 'some' usually has, the reasoning we should have had to use in answering our question would have been different. In the same way, if 'ought' means to us what it does when we are asking our moral questions, we shall have in our moral reasoning to follow the rules (of implication, consistency, etc.) determined by *that* meaning of the word (by the fact that it is *that* question we are asking, and not a different question which would be asked by someone who uttered the same sounds but was using 'ought' in another sense). It is therefore in order, if we wish to determine what rules we have to follow, to ask in what sense the word was being used in our question. Indeed, to ask in what sense it is being used *is* to ask what the rules are.

All this is peculiarly true of words like 'ought', one of the most general terms used in asking moral questions. Such words, like other modal words, express *formal* concepts, in the sense that the rules for their use are exhausted by the implications and other logical properties that they give to the propositions containing them. This is not true of all words: for example, the formal logical properties of the words 'blue' and 'red' are the same, but 'red' does not mean the same as 'blue'. So their formal logical properties cannot exhaust their meaning. But if 'ought' is a purely formal word, then we should be able to discover all there is to be known about its meaning and the rules for its use by studying its logical properties. If true, this is, as we shall see, of fundamental importance for ethics. It means that, although in a sense it has semantical properties as well (its 'descriptive meaning'), these are not part of its meaning in the narrow sense (H 1986c), and do not affect at all profoundly the rules for reasoning about what we ought to do.

The answer to the second objection mentioned at the beginning is thus that, because the concepts studied by ethics are formal, there do not have to be moral facts in the world in order for us to develop a theory of moral reasoning, any more than there have to be logical facts to substantiate logical reasoning. The necessities which constrain our reasoning are formal necessities—which does not mean, any more than it does in logic and mathematics, that they cannot *in conjunction with* substantial non-moral information about the world, help us in deciding moral questions of substance. How this is to be done, we shall see later.

1.3. It is now time to ask how we can discover what these formal properties are. The first step requires us to anatomize language as a whole in order to see where in the anatomy such words as 'ought' belong. The most perspicuous way of doing this is by speech act theory. The term 'speech act' was brought into currency by J. L. Austin (1962: 41, 149), though he does not himself use the term very much, preferring more specific expressions. He can justly be regarded as the founder of speech act theory; but the idea that not all speech acts are of the same kind or obey the same rules has been used before and after him by Wittgenstein, Ryle, Searle, Habermas, and many others. In order to divide off speech acts of different kinds from one another, we need to articulate the sentences that are used to perform them. The main purpose of this is, if possible, to isolate the features of sentences which perform the various functions necessary for a complete speech act. Then we can see which features of a sentence are peculiar to a particular kind of speech act, and so mark the utterance of it as a performance of that kind of speech act; and which features are common to a number of different kinds of speech act. The best known marker of this sort is the sign of mood (e.g. indicative or imperative) which (to speak generally at first) marks off statements from imperations (if we may use that expression for speech acts typically expressed in the imperative).

We also need to be clear that the division of speech acts into kinds takes the form of a tree with genera, species, sub-species, etc. It cannot be assumed, for example, that there are no further subdivisions within the classes of statements and imperations, nor that imperations may not belong, perhaps with moral judgements, within a larger class of prescriptions. Nor can it be assumed that a kind of speech act has to belong to one or other of these classes and cannot belong to more than one. The species and genera may not be mutually exclusive: perhaps moral judgements share some of the properties both of statements and of prescriptions. All this has to be investigated by the study of speech and language (I use these words to mark the distinction made famous by Saussure 1916).

A further necessary clarification can conveniently be made at this point. Austin used the term 'illocutionary force' to connote the property which distinguishes one speech act from another. Thus the statement that you are going to shut the door has a different illocutionary force from the command that you shut the door. But different writers since Austin have interpreted this distinction in different ways. Consider the two commands, that you open the door, and that you shut the window. Do these have the same illocutionary force, in that they are both commands, or different illocutionary forces, because they are different commands? It will make no difference to any argument, provided that we are clear about our use of the terms; but in what follows I shall myself adopt the second of these uses. I shall speak of these two commands as having two different illocutionary forces, though they belong to the same *type* of illocutionary force, namely the imperative. Similarly I can make two different statements, which have different illocutionary forces because their content is different, but have the same type of illocutionary force, namely what Austin called the constative (1962: 6 n.). This will be brought out if the sentences are articulated in such a way (as they are in most languages) as to distinguish the feature which marks the mood from the rest; the two commands 'Open the door' and 'Shut the window' share this feature, by which we recognize them as imperatives; but otherwise they differ.

The articulation of sentences, or the speech acts that they express, has to distinguish at least four functions (H 1989a). The first is the mood, already mentioned. I shall call the sign of mood the *tropic*. That mood is, or can be, part of meaning is evident from the fact that the Latin expressions '*i*' and '*ibis*' ('Go' and 'You are going to go') have different logical implications (H 1996*b*): the latter implies that you are going to leave this place; the former does not, because a command is not a prediction of its own fulfilment. Next, we have to distinguish the content of the speech act (for example what in particular is being stated to be the case, or commanded to be made the case). Thus the commands 'Open the door' and 'Shut the window' have the same tropic but different *phrastics* (using that term to denote the feature of the sentence, not necessarily a separate part of it, that indicates what is being e.g. stated or commanded). In a completely and perspicuously articulated language these functions would be assigned to different parts of the sentence.

The remaining two functions, which do not need to be discussed here, are those which would be expressed in a fully articulated language by the *clistic*, or sign of completeness, of the sentence, and the *neustic* or sign of subscription to a speech act by a speaker or writer. These signs are controversial, and many writers have denied the necessity of the latter in particular; but I shall not need to defend them for the purposes of the present argument (see H 1989*a*). Nevertheless, it is very important to distinguish between these different functions, as many writers (including myself in early days) have not (H 1971*c*: 21 ff.). In particular the tropic or mood-sign has to be distinguished from the neustic or sign of subscription, because one can mention or embed an indicative or imperative sentence, including its mood-sign, or use it mimetically (6.4, H 1989*a*)—e.g. on the stage—without making a statement or giving a command.

It will be asked at this point whether mood, as I am using the word, is a logical or a grammatical term. The answer is that it is both, but that we have to understand the difference between what are now often called surface and deep grammar, and used to be called grammatical form and logical form. If there is a difference between these two ways of making the distinction, it will not affect what I am now going to say. In history, grammar and logic grew up together, and metaphysics with them; and it has proved difficult to draw clear distinctions between these three. Even such diverse thinkers as Hegel and Carnap found it hard to distinguish between logic and metaphysics (Hegel assimilating the former to the latter, and Carnap, in effect, the reverse—though he reserved the name 'metaphysics' for what I have called 'mephistics'). And similarly deep grammar and logic are so intimately bound up with each other that it would be foolish to try to prise them apart. The difference between logic and surface grammar is what has made people think that there is a difference between grammar and logic as a whole.

There are indeed grammatical distinctions that have no logical significance, like that between strong and weak forms of the past tense (3.3). But mood is not like this; the distinction between the mood-sign and the rest of a sentence is as important logically as that between subject and predicate. These two have been both grammatical and logical terms, and rightly, because the grammar is a way of expressing the logic. In order to speak grammatically we have to be able to make, at any rate implicitly, the logical distinction; and when structural linguists construct their 'trees' (which in my school days was called 'parsing'), they are using the logical distinction in order to mark off noun-phrases from verb-phrases.

There are complications here into which I shall not be able to go—for example, the false thesis held by many, including Aristotle (*An. Pr.* 43ᵃ30), that there are terms which can occupy either subject or predicate places in propositions at will. The truth is that in 'Red is a primary colour' and 'The book is red', the word 'red' means different things, as is shown by the fact that we could rewrite the first sentence 'The colour red is a primary colour', but could not rewrite the second 'The book is the colour red'. Similarly, in 'Callias is a man' we can substitute 'human' for 'man'; but in 'Man is an animal' we cannot. As we have seen, if we alter the mood of a sentence, then by making the grammatical change we alter both its meaning and its logical properties; and this is enough to show that mood is both a logical and a grammatical category, without in this context distinguishing the two functions.

1.4. It is time to turn back to the question of what place moral judgements occupy in the anatomy of language, presuming that we have an adequate one. If it is adequate, it will at least distinguish between two genera of speech acts that I shall call the descriptive and the prescriptive (1.6). All kinds of ordinary statements will belong to the former, and all speech acts which are typically expressed in the imperative to the latter. We must not presuppose that nothing except imperations belongs to the latter genus. We must not even presuppose that in order to give a command it is necessary to use the imperative. But let us now ask in a preliminary way whether moral judgements (for example those expressed with 'ought') are prescriptive or descriptive speech acts. The answer is that they are both, but that the distinction needs to be carefully preserved, because otherwise we shall not be able to understand the *different* features of 'ought'-sentences which link them to the two genera.

'Ought'-judgements are prescriptive, and in this respect like imperations, because in their typical uses agreement with them, if genuine, requires action in conformity with them, in situations where the action required is an action of the person agreeing. I deliberately say 'in their typical uses', because, as is well known, there are other uses, which have generated a vast literature. Such are uses by the weak-willed person, 'acratic' or 'backslider' who does not do what he agrees he ought to, because he very much wants not to (H 1963*a*: ch. 5, 1992*e*: ii. 1304), and by the 'satanist' who does what he agrees he ought not to, just because it is what he ought not to (H 1992*d*: 98). This is not the place to add to this literature; the point here is just that typical and central uses of 'ought' require compliance if they are to count as sincere. By contrast, constative speech acts require only accordant belief.

However, moral judgements are not just like ordinary imperations. They share with constative speech acts a very important feature, namely that when I say 'I ought to do that', I have to say it because of *something about* the act that I say I ought to do. This is a feature of all uses of 'ought', and not just of moral uses. It is true that imperations too are normally issued for reasons. But they do not have to be. If a drill serjeant is trying to see whether a new recruit will obey him, he may say to him 'Right turn', and may have no reason at all for saying this rather than 'Left turn'. But with 'ought' it is different. To take a non-moral example: suppose that instead they are doing a tactical exercise and the instructor says 'You ought to attack on the right'. There has to be a reason in the facts of the situation why they ought to attack on the right rather than on the left (*FR* 3.3).

It is hard for Germans to appreciate this point, because the German word 'soll' can be used to translate both the English 'is to' (which can be equivalent to an imperative), and the English 'ought to' (which is a moral or other normative expression). Systems of deontic logic have sometimes been set up which fail to make this distinction, using a single symbol (for example 'O') for both 'ought' and the imperative. Since the logical behaviour of these is different (for example a 'square of opposition' which works for 'ought' does not work for imperatives—H 1967*d*), such systems start on the wrong foot. Confusion on this point can sometimes lead to treating the fact that one is commanded to do something (one *is to* or *soll* act in a certain way) as showing that one *ought* to act in that way. This can have grave political consequences (H 1955*b*).

Because moral judgements have to be made for reasons, the reasons being the facts of the situation, it is irrational to issue one having no regard for the facts (contrast the serjeant's command in the above example, which in no way convicts the serjeant of irrationality). It is indeed true that the choices expressed by imperative speech acts are normally required to be made for reasons if the chooser is not to be called irrational (H 1979*a*), and that even in this unusual case the serjeant *has* a reason for saying what he says (namely the intention to test the obedience of the recruit). But in this case he could have said 'Left turn' instead of 'Right turn' with equal rationality. It is the privilege of serjeants not to have reasons for this kind of choice.

Moral and other normative judgements by contrast cannot be arbitrary in this way. They have to be made because of the facts. This does not mean that the moral judgement *follows logically from* the facts (H 1963*b*: sec. 8). The facts do not *force* us logically to make one moral judgement rather than another; but, if we make one about one situation, we cannot, while admitting that the facts are the same in another situation, in the same breath make a conflicting one about the second situation. In the non-moral tactical example just used, the officer could not say that there might be another tactical situation just like this one in which they ought to attack on the left rather than on the right. If the facts are just the same, they would supply a reason for making the same normative judgement. This is the basis for the feature of normative judgements called *universalizability* (H 1963*a*: ch. 2), and moral judgements share this feature (1.7).

1.5. Before assigning to moral judgements their place on this anatomy, there is an important distinction to be made, which in spite of a very clear statement of it by Austin (1962: chs. 9, 10), is still neglected by many, especially in connection with imperations. It is encouraged by a too easy use of the term 'pragmatics' (6.5), and of the Wittgensteinian linking of meaning to use, by those who are not very clear about what exactly they mean by 'use' (see Austin 1962: 104). Austin distinguished between illocutionary and perlocutionary acts (6.4), the first being what we are doing *in* saying something (*in locutione*), and the second what we are doing or seeking to do *by* saying something (*per locutionem*). The 'pragmatics' and the 'use' of utterances are easily taken to mean the latter, especially in the case of imperatives; and so people slip into thinking that their meaning can be fully explained by giving their pragmatics or use, understanding by this their intended perlocutionary effect.

Besides the temptation just mentioned, there are others. Many logicians still hold the view, in spite of Austin and Wittgenstein, that there is only one kind of language-game or speech act that is respectable enough to be worthy of their attention, namely the constative. They sometimes cite Aristotle in their support (*De Int.* 16^{b}33 ff.). Others are so attached to truth-table and similar methods for setting up a logic that they cannot see how one could be set up that dealt with anything but true-or-false propositions. Others wish to define 'valid inference' as 'inference of such a form that no inference of that form can have true premisses and a false conclusion'.

Such writers exhibit the same sort of prejudice as has been in evidence in connection with the truth-condition theory of meaning. But there are many other ways of setting up logics, in particular that which starts from the notion of inconsistency. If we knew how to tell which speech acts were inconsistent with which, we could construct a logic for those kinds of speech acts. And imperations can certainly be inconsistent with one another (for example 'Shut the door' and 'Do not shut the door'). The inconsistency lies here within what I have called the phrastic, which the imperative shares with its corresponding indicative; so the source of inconsistency is the same for both, and therefore so is the nature of the logical fault. In this case, though not always (*LM* 2.3, Searle and Vanderveken 1985: 152), the sign of negation is part of the phrastic. But there is nothing here to make us banish imperative speech acts from logic. Indeed, the rules of logic itself, for example formation rules and rules of inference, are imperations, and *they* have to be consistent.

But the greatest temptation to this way of thinking about imperations (that they have only pragmatics and no logic) is a confusion between illocutionary and perlocutionary acts. Here it is necessary to depart from Austin's view. He distinguished between *three*, not just two, kinds of act, the third being the locutionary (Austin 1962: 108). But if he thought that only the locutionary act had meaning—and I have argued elsewhere that this is a misinterpretation (H 1971*c*: 115 ff.)—he was clearly wrong; for, as we have seen, mood is part of meaning ('Go' and 'You are going to go' do not mean the same). Therefore, in order to understand what somebody meant, we have to know what mood his speech act was in. And this is to know something about its illocutionary force. It is therefore incoherent to say, both that locutionary acts are the sole repositories of meaning, and that one can specify the locutionary act without mentioning its illocutionary force. Meaning is, in part, illocutionary act potential (Alston 1964: 37 ff.). This does not necessarily imply that other elements in the illocutionary force cannot extend beyond the locutionary act as specified. It has been alleged, for example, that we could know what a person meant when he said 'The ice is thin', and thus know what locutionary act he performed, without knowing whether he intended it with the illocutionary force of a warning or a mere statement of fact. I would dispute this, but it would need too long an excursus into such notions as warning to settle the matter. I deal with 'warn' briefly in 3.3. It can at any rate be granted that, as Austin (1962: 32, 69) pointed out, there are often ways of making the illocutionary force of our utterances explicit and thus disambiguating the sentence. We can do this by saying either 'I warn you that the ice is thin' or 'I affirm that the ice is thin'.

Be that as it may, the locutionary and illocutionary acts lie together on the other side of an important divide from the perlocutionary. For perlocutionary acts there can be no logic in a strict sense. The reason is that, as we have seen, logic is determined by the rules or conventions for the use of words, and perlocutionary acts (what we are doing or trying to do by saying things) need not be controlled by any rules or conventions of a logical sort (cf. Austin 1962: 118). It is true that what we can do by saying something depends on what the something is—i.e. on what we are doing in saying it—but it depends on much else; we have to size up the situation and think what would be the likely effects of certain utterances. Telling someone that the ice is thin may be a way of getting him not to go on the ice; but if he is a daredevil who does not fear cold water it may be a way of getting him to go on it. If he is a normal person who trusts us, it may be a way of getting him to believe that it is thin; if he is untrusting or countersuggestible, it may be a way of getting him to believe that it is not thin. And similarly with imperatives. Say 'Go on the ice' to a trusting child, and he may go; but say it to an untrusting or rebellious one, and it may make him do the opposite. Thus the same illocutionary act with the same meaning may have different perlocutionary effects, and this in itself shows that the perlocutionary effect or intended effect is not part of the meaning.

What may be called the 'verbal shove' theory of the meaning of imperatives has therefore to be rejected (*LM* 1.7, H 1971*c*: 91 ff., 6.3). If 'pragmatics' is taken confusedly to cover both illocutionary and perlocutionary acts, we can say that to study the meaning of imperatives is to study their pragmatics; but only the illocutionary part of their pragmatics at the most. If we stray beyond this, we are no longer studying their meaning at all. Once we realize this, we shall not include as imperations speech acts which are clearly statements, such as 'There is dust on the table' said by a demanding lady to her housemaid. It has been alleged that this is really an imperation, because it is intended to *get* the housemaid to dust the table. It may indeed be so intended; but that does not make it an imperation. It is a statement, which, in conjunction with an assumed standing order of the house (which *is* an imperation) that when tables are dusty she is to dust them, entitles the housemaid to infer the imperation that she is to dust the table. So, if the housemaid is both logical and obedient, saying this will get her to dust the table. But she has understood the meaning of the utterance perfectly well even if she is not obedient, and even if she has not heard of the standing order, and even if she is too stupid to think that there might be one. If she is stupid enough, she may not dust the table even if the tone of her mistress is menacing. She will not know what to do, because she has not been told that.

1.6. The relevance of all this to ethics is this. Moral judgements are, in a sense to be explained later, prescriptive, and therefore akin in some respects to imperations. The school of moral philosophers called *emotivists* (further discussed in Chapter 6) realized this. But, infected with the confusion about pragmatics that I have just been exposing, they were led into the error of thinking that the meaning of moral judgements had to be explained in terms of their perlocutionary effect (Urmson 1968: 29 ff.). This is evident from the title of the part of Stevenson's *Ethics and Language*, 'Pragmatic Aspects of Meaning' (1945: 37), which sets the tone for the whole book. But the same thought is to be found in Ayer (1936: ch. 6), and seems to be implicit in Carnap (1935: 23). It led people to look for the source of the meaning of imperations, and therefore of part of that of moral judgements, in their power of *getting* people to do things. But the perlocutionary act of getting them to do something is a quite different thing from the illocutionary act of telling them to do it (H 1951*a*). As we have seen, the latter may be a means of achieving the former; but this does not make them the same act in the sense relevant here. In particular, the illocutionary act of *telling to* is subject to logical control, just like the illocutionary act of *telling that*. In telling to, one must not contradict oneself, any more than in telling that; otherwise one is not telling people to do anything that they can do. But in getting to, including getting to believe that, one may contradict oneself if that is the most effective way of doing it.

The emotivists thus confused the essentially irrational or arational

perlocutionary act with the logic-governed illocutionary act. (6.3 f.)
So they not only thought without good reason that there could be no
logic of imperations, but, because of this confusion, tainted moral
judgements with the same irrationality. I have even heard it argued
that, because moral judgements are material for rational thought
and imperatives are not, moral judgements cannot be imperatives.
But the boot is on the other foot. Because imperations have to obey
logical rules, the fact that moral judgements share some of their
properties is no obstacle at all to the rationality of moral thinking.
Therefore rejections of non-descriptivist ethical theories by aspiring
rationalists on the ground that moral judgements could not be
rational unless they were statements in the narrow sense—or constative, to use Austin's term (1962: 6 n.)—miss the point entirely. It
can be allowed that in certain senses moral judgements can be called
true or false (H 1976b); but even if they could not, their rationality
would not be impugned. We shall see later that the prescriptivity of
moral judgements, so far from being a bar to their rationality, is a
vital ingredient in it (1.8).

But before showing this, it is time to ask in what sense moral
judgements are prescriptive, and how their prescriptivity combines
with their other features. And this cannot be clarified until we have
explained what prescriptivity is. We have already used the word to
describe the genus of speech acts to which imperations belong; they
are the paradigm of it. The simplest way of characterizing this genus
is to say that a speech act is prescriptive if someone who assents to it
is not being sincere if he does not act accordingly (i.e. at the time and
in the way specified), when he is the person whom it charges with fulfilling it, and is physically and psychologically able to do so (LM 2.2).
But there are some ambiguities here which need to be unravelled.
Expressions like 'the subject' and 'the addressee' (of an imperation)
can mean three different things. They may denote the person to
whom an imperation is spoken or written. Or they may denote the
person or thing to which the grammatical subject of the sentence
used refers. Or they may mean the person charged with complying
with the imperation. These may all be different persons or things. If
the *grande dame* in our previous example says to her butler 'The table

is to be dusted', the grammatical subject refers to the table; the person spoken to is the butler; and the person who is charged with complying is the housemaid (butlers do not dust tables).

In the present context it is the person charged that interests us. Let us call her, not the addressee or the subject, but the chargee. A prescriptive speech act is one such that, if I am the chargee, and I assent to the speech act, I cannot be assenting sincerely if I do not act accordingly. For example, if the above command is addressed to the housemaid, who knows that she is the person charged with dusting tables when they are to be dusted, and she assents by saying 'Very good, madam', she is not assenting sincerely if, though she could dust the table, she at once slinks off to bed without dusting it.

1.7. Are moral judgements prescriptive in this sense? Certainly not all are. The housemaid can assent to the judgement (even taken in a moral sense) that she ought to dust the table, and still slink off to bed. The question is rather, 'Is there an important class of moral judgements which *is* prescriptive, and if so what is the relation between those that are and those that are not?' It can be argued (but not here) that Plato (see H 1982*a*: 56, 66), Aristotle (*Eth. Nic.* 1143^{a}8, 1147^{a}25 ff.), Hume (1739: III. 1. 1), Kant (*Gr* BA36 f. = 412 f.) and Mill (1843: last chapter) all thought that moral judgements were typically prescriptive, though probably none of these thought that all were, nor that this exhausted their meaning, any more than I do (H 1998*a*). I have argued elsewhere that there is a prescriptive use of moral judgements, and that this is central in two senses. The first is that, if this use is explained, the others can be explained in terms of it and fall into place (*LM* ch. 11). The second is that, as I shall be saying later, their prescriptivity is a vital ingredient in moral reasoning (1.7; *MT* 6.1).

It was his recognition, inherited from Socrates and Plato, that moral and other normative judgements are prescriptive, that made acrasia or weakness of will a problem for Aristotle. If they are prescriptive, how could the housemaid assent to one and then slink off to bed? If Aristotle had been a pure descriptivist, as some of his pretended modern followers seem to themselves to be, there would have been no problem for him in the housemaid's backsliding. He devotes half a book to resolving the Socratic problem (*Eth. Nic.* 1145^{b}21 ff.), because he, like Socrates, has to explain how one can accept a prescription and then not act on it. His explanation, though not completely adequate, is more subtle than that of Socrates. It consists in pointing out that the prescription in question is universal (the housemaid knows she ought to dust the table because she knows the universal rule of the household, and all households that are well ordered, that dusty tables ought to be dusted, and knows the particular fact that this table is dusty). Though his example is different, Aristotle could say that she can backslide from the universal rule because she is tired and wants to go to bed, and therefore ignores the particular fact, even though it is evident enough. This summary does not do justice to the subtlety of his solution to the problem, and I have myself suggested a more complex solution (*FR* ch. 5, H 1992*e*: ii. 1304). But the important thing is that there is a problem, which there would not be if we were descriptivists.

If, in spite of this alleged difficulty, we recognize that central cases of moral judgements are prescriptive, we still have to recognize also that they are not *purely* prescriptive. That indeed is the major part of the more complex solution to the problem of acrasia. As Aristotle (*Eth. Nic.* 1147^{a}31) and Kant (*Gr* sec. 2, para. 31) both saw, moral judgements are not merely prescriptive but *universally* prescriptive. And the universality of the moral prescription easily introduces a non-prescriptive element into its meaning. To explain this: if the housemaid accepts the universal rule that dusty tables ought to be dusted, this rule will assume for her (obedient girl as she normally is) the status of fact. That is, if ever she is tempted (as now) to neglect her duty, she will not be able to avoid thinking of the possibility that her mistress or the butler will notice the omission and punish her; and, if they do, *that* is a real enough fact. And so is the fact that she is frightened by the thought. Some people's attitude to morality is like that of the housemaid to the butler. Even when the housemaid has left that (or all) employment and has a house of her own—even when there is no longer a *grande dame* and the butler is out of work—she will not be able to escape the feeling of guilt caused in her by the sight of a dusty table for which she is responsible.

It is easy for the irreligious to proceed from this analogy to the thought that God does not exist, and that therefore everything is permitted. They should reflect on two things. The first is that, God or no God, the attitudes that make us revere the laws of morality are a social necessity; we could not live in communities without them. Kant may have carried this reverence to excess, and his moral law was no doubt too simple and rigid. But society would collapse unless children were brought up to feel bad when they do bad things; and we should not let psychologists convince us otherwise without empirical evidence to the contrary. The second is that a reflective critical morality can *justify* these laws or rules or principles and our attitudes to them. So even if there were no *grande dame* we would have to invent her. Critical moral thinking can also amend the principles if they are seen to be unsuited to our situation (*MT* 3.3).

The inescapable factuality or descriptivity of moral principles has a logical as well as a psychological basis (*MT* ch. 2). Moral judgements are like factual statements in many respects (on the face of it, they resemble each other more than either of them resembles imperations). It is easy, therefore, to think that they are like them in all respects. It is made easier still by the existence of a large class of moral judgements, referred to above, which are not prescriptive. The similarity is so great that I have thought it right to follow Stevenson (1945: 62 ff.) in using the term 'descriptive meaning' for the element in the meaning of moral judgements that makes them like constative speech acts. This is not the same as the *phrastic* referred to above (1.3); that is something else, which would indeed be part of moral judgements even if they were plain imperations, which they are not.

The element I am calling descriptive meaning can best be indicated by a non-moral example borrowed from Urmson (1968: 133). If you are meeting a girl at the station and do not know her by sight, I may enable you to recognize her by saying, among other things, that she has a good figure. To say this is to describe her, and my purpose has nothing to do with prescribing the acquisition of such figures. We all know what in our society counts as a good figure, so you will know what to look for. If your informant were a member of a society that thought fat girls more attractive, you would look for a different sort of figure. Thus the descriptive meaning of 'good figure' is different in the two societies.

Because the standards or criteria for commendation vary from society to society and from century to century, whether we are speaking of moral or of other kinds of commendation, the descriptive meaning of words like 'good', 'right', 'wrong', and 'ought' can be relied on only within a certain circle; but within that circle it is reliable enough. Other evaluative and normative words have their descriptive meaning so firmly tied to them that it is hard to use them in communication between different societies; so that, if we were confined to the latter class of words (for example 'blasphemous' and 'cruel'), we might not be able to talk about values to those who did not substantially share our own values. We should have to fight one another. It is the existence of shared general value-words like 'ought' that makes peaceful discussion between cultures possible (H 1986c, 1993g, 6.9).

Moral judgements acquire a descriptive meaning, even without butlers to enforce them, because of an important logical feature that they share with other value judgements, called *universalizability* (*FR* 2.2). One way of approaching this is to say that all such judgements are made for reasons: that is, because of *something about* the subject of the judgement. The girl's figure could not be good if it were not good because of something about her measurements. A man cannot be a good man, if not because of the sort of man he is. An act cannot be wrong, if not because of something about it. They cannot be good or wrong just because they are good or wrong; there must be properties other than their goodness or wrongness which make them so. This feature of value judgements is sometimes called 'supervenience'. Causal judgements have it too: if an event causes another, there could not be a qualitatively identical situation in which the corresponding events were not conjoined and causally linked. This is the basis of the so-called 'covering law' theory of causal explanation (Hempel 1965: 345 ff.). And the notion has other applications too. But moral philosophers should not be misled by philosophers of mind and others who have borrowed the word and used it in another meaning which they have not made clear (H 1984b).

That moral properties supervene on non-moral properties means simply that acts, etc., have the moral properties because they have the non-moral properties ('It is wrong because it was an act of inflicting pain for fun'), although the moral property is not the same property as the non-moral property, nor even entailed by it. Someone who said that it was an act of inflicting pain for fun but not wrong would not be contradicting himself, though most of us would call him immoral. Logic does not forbid the adoption of different moral standards by different people; it simply prohibits a single person from adopting inconsistent standards at the same time, and says that they *will* be inconsistent if he says conflicting things about situations which he agrees to be identical in their universal properties.

1.8. It has been disputed whether the universalizability of moral judgements is a logical feature of them, or embodies a substantial moral principle. A ground for holding the former view is that we react to breaches of the principle in the same sort of way as to breaches of logical principles. If someone says that there are two situations identical in all their universal non-moral properties, but says he thinks that the protagonist in one ought to tell a lie, but the protagonist in the other ought not, we are likely to be as nonplussed as if he had said that he thought that a rotating disc was both stationary and not stationary (cf. Plato, *Rep.* 436d). In either case there could be an explanation. In the second he might mean that the axis of rotation was stationary, so that the disc continued to occupy the same region of space, but that within this region it moved around its axis.

In the first case there could be many explanations, but none of them would impugn the universalizability thesis. The protagonists in the two cases might themselves have different characteristics. But when the thesis speaks of identical situations, it must be understood as ruling out this difference too. Another possibility is that in one case the person to be lied to is the mother of the protagonist, and in the other not. One can only have one (genetic) mother, and it might be thought that this makes a difference, because to tell lies to one's mother is worse than if someone else tells them to a person (perhaps even the same person) who is not his mother, however similar the situations. But relations can be universal properties (5.8), and the relation *being the mother of* is one such. The situations are different in respect of a universal relational property, because in one the liar and the person to be lied to are related as mother to child, and in the other not.

Examples like this force us to make clear what the thesis means by 'universal property'. A simple, but for our present purposes sufficient, definition is the following. A property is universal if, in order to specify it, it is not necessary to mention any individual (for an apparent exception, in which the expression referring to the individual is preceded by 'like' or its equivalent, see 5.8 and *FR* 2.2).

It is sometimes claimed that the thesis of universalizability is inconsistent with the principle of the identity of indiscernibles. For it claims that, if there were two situations identical in all their universal properties, the same moral judgements would have to be made about both; but the principle of the identity of indiscernibles holds that there cannot be two situations, numerically different, but identical in all their universal properties. However, it has been convincingly argued that in this extreme form the principle of the identity of indiscernibles is not true (e.g. Strawson 1959: 119). It is true in less extreme forms, e.g. if it claims only that things identical in all their universal properties *and* in their relations to individuals must be numerically identical; but this obviously causes no trouble to the universalizability thesis.

There is a further problem about whether being actual as opposed to merely possible or hypothetical is a universal property (*MT* 6.4). If it were, a form of special pleading would become possible in moral reasoning, by which an aggressor could claim that he would never be actually in the position of his victim, and that this difference was morally relevant. It is perhaps best to follow those (e.g. Lewis 1973: 85) who claim that the actual world cannot be distinguished from possible worlds without a reference to individuals, namely those who are actual; but not to follow them into thinking that possible worlds have some real existence in limbo. In any case it seems that making moral distinctions on the ground of actuality would be rejected on logical grounds as we use words like 'ought'. If someone said 'I ought in the actual case, but someone else ought not in an identical hypothetical case', we should not understand what moral principle he was invoking, because a moral principle which applied to the actual case but not to hypothetical cases exactly like it would not be counted by us as a moral principle, whatever our substantial moral views were, nor as any other sort of normative principle. This problem has analogies with the old one of whether existence is a property.

Those who think that the universalizability thesis is a substantial moral principle and not a logical doctrine will by this time be getting restive. They will think that we have fixed the logic so as to enable us to reach substantial conclusions in moral arguments. We must ask them to be patient until we have explained how the arguments work. Until then we can only point out that we would object to the above conjunction of moral judgements about the actual and hypothetical cases even if we knew nothing whatever about the substantial moral opinions of the person who made them; so it cannot be anything substantial that we are objecting to. The objection must therefore be logical. Suppose, even, that he also says that on other grounds he believes in complete impartiality between people, himself and others. It is not inconsistent to believe in impartiality between people, and still try to call the difference between actual and hypothetical morally relevant; for if it were relevant it could be used impartially between people. So we cannot be introducing a substantial moral principle requiring impartiality between people by insisting that actuality is not a morally relevant feature. On the problem of moral relevance in general see H 1978*b*: 73, *MT* 3.9.

We have found reasons for thinking that the universalizability thesis is a logical and not a substantial moral doctrine. The main ground on which people have thought otherwise is that the thesis does seem to have implications of a substantial sort for moral arguments, and there is some suspicion of a conjuring trick—of producing a substantial moral rabbit out of a logical hat. Moral philosophers have so often attempted similar tricks that one is right to be suspicious. For example they have sought to attribute a certain meaning on logical or conceptual grounds to phrases such as 'human needs', and have then gone on to extract substantial moral principles from these definitions (4.6). How we can allay this suspicion will not be clear until we have set out more fully the argument from formal logical or philosophy-of-language considerations to an account of substantial morality. Here we must simply note that formal considerations are only one element in moral arguments. Others are the facts about situations, which are substantial, and in particular facts about people's *wills*, to use Kant's word; and these facts too are substantial (8.5 f.).

Let us try out this essentially Kantian method more clearly, and relate it to its basis in philosophy of language. If moral judgements are prescriptive, as has been argued, then in making one, I am asking that it be acted on, and, if sincere, must will this. But if they are also universalizable, I am, in making one, implicitly making identical judgements for all situations identical in their universal properties, no matter what role particular individuals, including myself, occupy in them. The question of what moral prescriptions I am prepared to issue thus resolves itself into that of what I am prepared to will for all situations of a given kind, no matter what role I occupy. Thus to issue a moral prescription I must accept the consequences (even the hypothetical consequences) of its being obeyed whatever role I occupy.

How constrictive this is will depend on what I will should be done to myself, were I in those various roles. The roles include the fact that the wills of the people in them are what they are. If I were in those situations, my will would in each case be the same as the present will of the person who is now in it, since the willing is part of the situation. So the question resolves itself into that of what I now will (NB not what I *would* will) should be done to me in those situations, in which I willed what they now will.

But here another factor enters, also obtainable from the logic of our language. By an argument which does not invoke universalizability, we can see that I must have as much regard to what I would will in those situations, as I do to what I now will. For if I do not, I am either not representing the situations fully to myself, or else not thinking of the person in them as *myself* (7.3, *MT* 5.4). To think of him as myself is to identify myself with his will. This is part of what we *mean* by 'myself'. Reflection on the meaning of 'myself' should convince us of this. The case is analogous to what I think about *future* states of myself which I expect to be actual. If I know what I shall then will, and am really thinking of the person in the situation as *myself*, and do not irrationally discount the future, my will must be as strongly engaged as that of the future person who will be me. If anybody doubts this, he should arrange for himself to be whipped, and reflect on his state of mind just before it happens (cf. Aristotle, *Eth. Nic.* 1115ᵃ24). Failure to engage my will in this way is always due either to a failure of representation of the situation of the person that I shall be, or to a failure to think of him (or her) as *myself*.

Since for moral argument hypothetical situations are as relevant as actual, I have to will that the same should be done to me in them too. They will include all the situations in which I would occupy the roles of those affected by proposed actions of mine. I am therefore faced with the problem of finding a universal prescription for situations like that which I am presently in, which I can accept equally for all the identical situations that I could be in, in different roles. This in effect gives equal weight in my moral thinking to the wills of all those affected by my actions. The Kingdom of Ends is not really a kingdom, but a democracy with equality before the law. But if all wills have equal weight in proportion to their strength (for obviously how strong they are must make a difference) then the problem of doing justice between all these wills is to be resolved by choosing the moral prescription which maximally realizes the fulfilment of them, treating all impartially and giving them weight according to their strength (H 1996c).

1.9. This development of Kant's ideas thus turns into a kind of rational-will utilitarianism (see Chapter 8). He is, admittedly, selective with regard to the kinds of will that he is prepared to enfranchise: they have to be rational; but many utilitarians accept this. This shows the superficiality of the commonly accepted dogma that Kant and the utilitarians need to be at odds. If the two doctrines are sympathetically formulated, they are in agreement. The disagreement remaining is one *within* utilitarianism, as to whether any kinds of will are to be excluded from consideration. And such a formulation involves the use of insights from the philosophy of language. There is no space here to develop these insights further, nor to deal with other objections and difficulties. This must be left until later, and to my writings on the philosophy of education (e.g. H 1992d), in order to show how in practice we manage to find a level of moral thinking more suited to us humans than the somewhat demanding level in which Holy Wills can engage.

It was Kant's predicament in between these levels (dare we say his insufficient grasp of an important difference between the levels?) that led him to try to justify what are only simple, general, prima facie intuitive principles (suitable to our human condition) *directly* by appeal to the Categorical Imperative; and this notoriously got him into trouble (8.4). The right way to try to justify them would have been to show that a Holy Will (perhaps God, whom Kant would have liked to believe in) would, by a use of the Categorical Imperative as it would be used by such a supremely rational will, select these simpler principles for the guidance of less rational wills than his own. But 'we have no intuition of the divine perfection, but can only deduce it from our own conceptions' (*Gr* BA92 = 443). We have no direct access to what a good God would will, so we have recourse to our own imperfect reason as the best means available to us.

In conclusion, we have to ask, in deference to an earlier objector, whether this development of Kantian ideas relies on resources lying beyond the philosophy of language, and in particular on antecedent substantial moral ideas and intuitions. Kant called his most-read work on this subject *Grundlegung zur Metaphysik der Sitten*. What has been sketched in this chapter is a kind of *Grundlegung zur Logik der Sitten*; and, as we have seen (1.3), logic and metaphysics are hard to tell apart. It certainly does not seem as if we have relied on extra-logical premisses. Anyone who doubts this should look for them. The argument has been generated using the following elements: first, the prescriptivity of moral judgements; secondly, their universalizability; and thirdly, the thesis that fully to represent another's situation to oneself one must come to have a will similar to his (or hers) for a situation in which one occupies his role. The last of these elements was obtained by considering what full representation of a hypothetical situation means, and what it means to think of a person in it as myself. All these are conceptual or logical moves, not involving appeals to substantial moral intuitions. Although, therefore, they can all be disputed, the disputes will be within the philosophy of language, since the theses themselves belong to it. So at least we can claim to have shown the relevance of philosophy of language to ethics. But see 5.8 for further discussion of universalizability.

2

DEFENCE OF THE ENTERPRISE

2.1. THE best way to understand what moral philosophy is, and why anybody should wish to study it, will be to take a practical moral problem and find the points at which we seem to be raising philosophical questions in our discussion of it. If my experience is anything to go by, one cannot discuss any serious moral problem for more than about half an hour without some philosophical tangle emerging. I am not going to discuss in depth any practical moral issue; I have done that in many of my other writings, but there is not space for it here. I want just to show how philosophical questions arise; later we shall see how the various kinds of ethical theory try to deal with them (I give my own answers in 7.9). For this purpose a very sketchy example will do; but this is merely by way of illustration. I have done my bit for practical moral philosophy elsewhere.

The best example to take may be the one that got me myself into moral philosophy: the question of whether it is wrong to fight in wars and kill people. In 1938–9 I had to face the problem, and Americans had to face it at the time of the Vietnam War. It is a problem about which anybody who thinks seriously about moral questions has to make up his mind. I have written about it in H 1985*b*, *MT* 10.2, and elsewhere. The American experience illustrates more of the points that I want to raise than my own experience before the Second World War, because in the case of Vietnam one could hold a position according to which, though not in general a pacifist, one had moral objections to fighting in *this particular war*; and such objections were not in the United States, and would not have been in Britain, allowed as reasons for exemption from military service.

Let us then think about the problems facing a young American about to be drafted and sent to fight in Vietnam. Let us suppose that he is inclined towards, but not committed to, pacifist views; that, whether or not he accepts pacifism, he is quite sure that there is something wrong (something very hard to specify exactly) with his country's policies and actions in Vietnam; that however, even if it be agreed that America is doing something *morally* wrong in Vietnam, that by no means entails that *he* ought to refuse downright to be drafted, or take evasive action. For it might be that, although his country was doing wrong, *his* duty was to his country, right or wrong. Or, if that be thought too extreme or too old-fashioned a position, he might think that he was not in a position to judge of the complexities of world strategy, and that it was his duty to leave the decision to those who were better informed than himself. Or he might think that although, if one considers Vietnam in particular, America was doing something wrong, to rebel against one's country would be a greater evil than acquiescing in *this* degree of moral evil committed by one's government. He might be quite ready to admit that, if the American government were to become like the Nazis and embark on a policy of wholesale genocide (massacring all blacks, for example), it would be his duty to rebel against it; but he might be in doubt whether the United States' government's actions in Vietnam were of sufficient wickedness to justify him in refusing his normal duty as a citizen. But what is one's normal duty as a citizen?

2.2. I have done enough, perhaps, to illustrate the complexity of the issues that arise in such a choice-situation. There is no reason why I should have stopped where I did; I could easily have shown that in fact the issues are even more complex. But let us stop for a moment and try to sort out the complexities that we have encountered so far.

The first group of problems that we have to consider is that raised by the pacifist position. What is supposed to be wrong about going to war and fighting? We might feel inclined at once to answer that war and fighting are prima facie wrong because they involve killing or wounding people (to say nothing of the economic loss that often results from wars and the preparation for them). Most people would agree that in general one ought not to kill or wound people. But— and here is the difficulty—most people would also agree that there are particular cases in which it is legitimate to kill or wound people (in self-defence, for example). It is true, however, and important, that people could be found who would dissent from either of these two propositions to which I have said that most people would agree. There have been people (Nietzscheans, for example) who have argued that fighting is a good thing just because it results in the elimination of the weak and their domination by the strong, so that the race is thereby improved; and the killing and wounding of people is an essential part of the process. And there have been others (the followers of Tolstoy, for example, and certain Indian sects), who have maintained that absolutely all violence is illegitimate.

However, leaving aside for the present these two extreme positions, even the more moderate ones in between face us with enough problems. For if you think that in general killing or wounding people is wrong, you have on your hands the problem of what distinguishes the classes of case where it is legitimate from those in which it is not. And I do not see how, in principle, one could set out to answer *this* question without raising the prior question 'What *in general* makes it wrong to kill or wound?' For only if we know what is wrong about killing or wounding in general shall we be able to say in what particular cases this general wrongness of killing is either absent, or else outweighed by other considerations which are present in those cases.

2.3. If I may allow myself another piece of autobiography: it was when I saw, looming behind the particular question, 'Is it wrong to kill people in wars?', the much more general question, 'Why is it wrong to kill people anyway?', that I really took to moral philosophy in earnest. There are, after all, a whole lot of circumstances in which it would be, to say the least, convenient to kill people. In my youth I was much addicted to murder stories, and these provide plenty of illustrations of cases in which, for particular people, it would be highly convenient to kill other particular people. But those were not the cases I was primarily thinking of. I was thinking more of cases where even ordinary *bien pensants* citizens might be tempted to think that it would be convenient to get certain people out of the way.

Let us start with some very tempting cases. I was on a working party many years ago which was discussing the problem, which still vexes the media, and on which there have been important legal decisions recently—the problem of whether a person should in the following circumstances be allowed to die: he had an injury to his brain such that it could be safely predicted that he would never recover consciousness; but the lower centres of his brain were in perfectly good order, so that he could be kept alive indefinitely by intravenous artificial feeding. The question was, 'Was it legitimate to stop the artificial feeding?'

I may mention that, a long time after the working party, my own sister died of the effects of a stroke, and the same problem might easily have arisen (she was in fact unconscious for a month before she died), but mercifully it did not. It is interesting that Pope Pius XII, whose views were in general rather conservative, pronounced in an allocution that in such cases it was legitimate to cease to keep a patient alive artificially (*Acta Apostolicae Sedis* xxxix (1957): 1027–33). But this probably did not apply to artificial *feeding*. The working party on which I was sitting consisted of theologians, a distinguished ecclesiastical lawyer, some well-known doctors, and some philosophers. Its report was supposed to provide guidance to church people and others (especially the bishops in the House of Lords) when subjects like this come up.

I have sat on many such working parties, sponsored by the Church of England and lay institutions, including a more recent one on euthanasia proper. We had one on abortion which, I think, had some influence, and was helpful in securing the liberalization of the law in 1967. I shall not discuss any of these subjects at length now: I have myself published articles on them as well as subscribing to the reports of the working parties (e.g. H 1975c, d, 1988d, 1993d). On abortion, some people are prepared to argue as follows: it is always wrong to kill an innocent human being; but an abortion is killing an innocent human being; therefore abortion is always wrong. I do not think any of us on the working party were prepared to accept this simple argument. In our discussions, we of course considered the somewhat analogous case of the Belgian mother who killed her infant child who was born deformed as a result of thalidomide taken by her when pregnant. And more recently I have taken part in discussions and published an article on the treatment of spina bifida cases which raise a similar problem (H 1974b).

The main point to notice with all these problems is: unless one knows what it is that makes killing a normal adult human being wrong, one is unlikely to be able to answer with any assurance the question of whether killing a foetus, or killing a defective new-born baby, or killing at his or her request a terminal patient in agony, in these exceptional circumstances, shares those features which make it wrong to kill in the normal case.

This was essentially Socrates' point when, again and again in the dialogues of Plato, he would not allow anybody to say that he knew that some particular thing was good or bad or right or wrong or anything else, until he had been given a clear answer to the question '*What is it* to be good or bad, etc.?' However, we must be clearer than perhaps Socrates was about the distinction between two different questions. The one I have been asking throughout is '*What is wrong about*, for example, killing people?' This might be rephrased in the form 'What is it about killing people that makes it, in general, wrong?' We must distinguish this from the quite different though related question, 'How do we know, or how can we prove, that it is wrong?' Somebody might be quite sure about the answer to the question 'What makes it wrong to kill people?', but be still unable to say how he knew this. Both questions can, unfortunately, be expressed by means of the ambiguous formulation 'Why is it wrong to kill people?' This might mean 'What is it that makes it wrong?', or it might imply a question about how we know that it is wrong. The confusion between these two questions has got moral philosophers into a lot of trouble. Both questions are, of course, very important ones, and they are closely related to each other, but all the same distinct. And both are distinct from the question 'What does wrong *mean?*', though this too is related.

2.4. Once one gets talking about euthanasia of the incurably ill, one is naturally led on to think about the putting away of other people who are not actually ill, but merely socially a nuisance. This is an example of the 'slippery slope', or the 'thin end of the wedge', which has figured prominently in arguments on all these questions. People who use such arguments usually do not see what the trouble is. The trouble arises precisely because they have not considered what

I called the prior question of what makes killing wrong in general. So they are naturally at a loss when it comes to drawing the line between cases where killing is legitimate and where it is not. Such people should be recommended to answer the prior question. Then they might find it easier to draw the line, and find a footing on the slippery slope.

There has been a great deal of controversy recently, especially in the United States, about the death *penalty*. It may be that in times to come people will think the terms in which this controversy has been conducted terribly old-fashioned, and in particular the word 'penalty'. We think it was barbarous of our nineteenth-century ancestors to hang people for sheep-stealing or for destroying the heads of fishponds. Many people now think it barbarous to hang or otherwise execute murderers. But suppose we forget about all this old-fashioned talk of *crimes* and *penalties*, and look at the matter in an extremely practical way. We spend an enormous amount of money on prisons; the people in them do not have a nice time; sometimes they escape and endanger the public; a great many of them are either mentally abnormal or for some other reason unlikely ever to fit into society as useful citizens. So why not start systematically weeding out the hopeless cases? We should save a lot of money and effort, which might then be spent on greater endeavours to help the cases that are not hopeless.

This train of thought can go even further. There is some, though not conclusive, empirical evidence for the thesis that a substantial part of the causes which make people take to crime are genetic. If, as is not unlikely, we become able to identify these criminal factors early (for example, by watching people's behaviour at school, truancy being an obvious bad sign, which is said to be linked quite closely with later delinquency), why not weed out these not very hopeful specimens early, and concentrate our educational efforts on those boys and girls who have a good chance of turning into the sort of men and women we want to have in society?

I am not, needless to say, actually advocating such a policy, and I shall say why later (7.9). I have strayed rather far from the pacifist question with which I started. I wanted us to see how wide are the ramifications of the question of what is wrong with killing people. I think that in the next few years we shall have to devote a lot of thought to this problem. I want to show how moral philosophy enters into this sort of discussion—to indicate what is its bearing on this problem about killing people.

2.5. Any moral problem one cares to take is bound to be divisible into the following elements. There are first of all questions of fact. To take the example I have just been discussing: the question, whether the psychologists are right who say that it is possible to identify genetic elements in the causes of crime, is a question of fact, which can be investigated empirically. In most practical moral problems it will be found that the huge majority of the questions which have to be settled before we can solve them are factual ones. This has tempted some philosophers to think that the *only* questions that have to be answered before we can solve them are of this sort—that once all the facts are known, no further problem will remain; the answer to the moral question will be obvious. This is, however, not so, as we shall see in due course. But certainly the factual questions are the ones that cause 99 per cent of the trouble. We can see this if we study any two people arguing about a moral question. We shall nearly always find them disputing each other's facts. To revert for a moment to the problem of the draftee who has to decide whether to go into the army: most of his problem is to find out what is actually happening in, for example, Vietnam, and what the actual consequences of various courses of action, whether on his or his government's part, are likely in fact to be.

Nevertheless, it is fairly obvious that one might find out all the facts that anybody wanted to adduce, and still be in doubt what one ought to do. We can see this more clearly if we suppose that there are two draftees and they are arguing with one another about the question. It is obvious that they could agree, for example, that if they went into the armed forces and obeyed their orders, they would find themselves killing a lot of civilians in the course of attacks on military objectives. One of them might think it morally indefensible to kill civilians in the course of fighting (especially if the civilians had nothing to do with the fighting, but were innocent bystanders). The other might think that this, although in itself an evil, had to be done if necessary in order to secure some greater good. One can agree about a fact, but disagree about its bearing on a moral issue.

However, it is not at all clear what follows from this. Some philosophers have gone straight from this premiss to the conclusion that there are ineliminable judgements of value which are logically unrelated to questions of fact, so that one can agree about the facts but still disagree about these questions of value. And these people usually go on to say that one cannot argue about questions of value. All the argument one can do on a moral question consists in establishing the facts; once these are established one may still differ about questions of value. And then there is nothing one can do about it but agree to differ, or try to bring non-rational means of persuasion to bear on one another, or, in the last resort, fight one another.

There may be some element of truth in what these people say—I shall be asking in Chapter 6 whether there is. But I hope that it will be agreed that it is much too early to reach this conclusion. For we do not yet know how moral argument is *supposed* to proceed. If the opponents of the position I have just outlined maintain that, on the contrary, there *are* arguments which, starting from agreed facts as premisses, lead to value judgements as conclusions, we obviously cannot decide between them and their opponents unless we investigate the forms of argument by which, it is suggested, we can reach these conclusions. And in investigating these forms of argument we shall be doing moral philosophy.

2.6. How does one investigate forms of argument? This is supposed to be the task of logic; but what is logic? And can there be a branch of logic which deals with moral and other evaluative statements? By 'evaluative statements' or 'value judgements' I mean, for the time being, the class of statements which includes most moral judgements, or at any rate a central and typical class of them, and also other statements or judgements in which words like 'ought', 'right','good', and the like occur. This is of course an entirely vague and unsatisfactory characterization of the class of evaluative statements; it is also not comprehensive enough. For a more serious attempt to define 'evaluative', see FR 2.8.

If we said that there can be a logic which deals with evaluative statements, we should of course be begging the question at issue between those who say that there can be argument about questions of value and those who say that there cannot. For if there is a kind of logic which can deal with them, there can obviously be argument about them.

But how do we decide whether there can be a kind of logic which deals with a certain class of statements? Let us take a simple example. How do I know that there is a kind of logic that enables me to go from the premiss 'If *p* then *q*; and *p*' to the conclusion 'Therefore *q*'? Is it because one can find that kind of inference in all the logic books? But surely an appeal to the authority of logic books is not enough. They might be wrong. I cannot launch out now into a discourse on the nature of logical validity; but I will say very briefly what I think about this. We satisfy ourselves that the *modus ponens* form of inference is valid (*modus ponens* is the form of inference that I have just mentioned, from 'If *p* then *q*; and *p*' to 'Therefore *q*')—we satisfy ourselves that *modus ponens* is valid by satisfying ourselves that that is indeed how we use the word 'if'. That is to say, we satisfy ourselves that a person who admitted that if *p* then *q*, and that *p*, but denied that *q* would be *misusing* the word 'if'. To admit that if *p* then *q* is to admit the propriety of affirming *q*, once one has the additional information that *p*. If one then denies that *q*, although one admits that *p*, one can reasonably be asked whether one really *meant* 'If *p* then *q*'.

To take an even simpler example: suppose I say 'There is a dog in the garden', but then go on to deny that there is any animal in the garden. I can reasonably be asked 'How were you using the word "dog", then?' For 'dog' *means* one kind of animal. The validity of the inference 'There's a dog in the garden, therefore there's an animal in the garden' rests, plainly, on the meaning of the word 'dog'. In general, establishing the validity of logical inferences is establishing that we use the words in them in such a way that the conclusions really do follow from the premisses.

If, therefore, we are going to decide the question of whether there can be arguments having moral judgements as their conclusions or constituents, we have, inescapably, to ask whether the meanings of

the moral words like 'good' and 'ought' are such as to make arguments of this sort valid or possible. The study of logic leads on inevitably to the study of language. So in my first book I was rash
enough to *define* ethics as 'the logical study of the language of morals'
(*LM* Preface). For this I was taken to task, because it was thought that
I was abetting the diversion of the activities of moral philosophers
from substantial questions of morality to what were called *verbal*
questions. But I hope it will be clear by now that, if we are going to
have a hope of answering the substantial questions with any assurance, we shall have to tackle these verbal questions. *For unless we understand fully what we, or what the opponents in a moral argument, or in a
theoretical argument about morals, are saying, we shall never be able to decide rationally any of the questions that arise.*

So, therefore, alongside the factual questions that have to be answered before we can make any progress with a moral problem, there
has to be put another class of question: questions about the meanings of words. I have given the theoretical reason for this, namely that
all argument depends on logic, and what is or is not logically valid depends on what words mean. But I could equally well have quoted empirical evidence. If one looks at almost any moral argument, for
example those conducted in the correspondence columns of the
newspapers, one cannot help noticing, interspersed among the factual arguments that are brought forward, frequent instances where
the disputants are at cross-purposes owing to ambiguities in the use
of words. One of them, it may be, thinks that some fact which he has
established proves some moral conclusion; his opponent does not
think it proves anything of the kind. This may be a sign merely that
they were understanding words in different senses.

So in trying to solve a moral problem we have to get the facts
straight, and we have to be clear about the meanings of the words we
are using, including the moral words. Only when we have done that
will it be clear whether there are other questions that have to be answered which do not fall into either of these two classes. In particular,
only then will it be clear whether there is a residual class of ultimate
questions of value which are neither questions of fact nor questions
about the meanings of words, and on which we can go on disagree-

ing even when we have agreed about the facts and about the meanings of the words we are using.

So, really, investigation of the meanings of the moral words plays a key part in the study of moral problems. It is only by undertaking it that we shall understand what it is that we are arguing about in a moral argument. And it is only by undertaking it that we shall find out what steps in the argument, if any, are valid. Thus moral philosophy—the logical study of the language of morals—has an indispensable part to play in practical moral arguments. But it is also of great importance to establish, as only moral philosophy can do, whether *any* moral arguments are cogent—whether, that is to say, moral judgements are the sort of things one can argue about at all. And this too can only be done by studying the moral words and their logical properties.

2.7. All this is so clearly true that it really is surprising that many writers have attacked recent moral philosophers for discussing the moral words, as if they ought to have been discussing something else. Certainly Socrates started the subject off by insisting on a study of the moral words, as I have already mentioned. Aristotle says of him that he was 'busying himself with moral questions . . . and directing the mind for the first time to definitions' (*Met.* 987^{b}I ff.).

We might feel inclined to retort to those who attack moral philosophy in this way, that they dislike our studying the moral words and their meanings because they do not *want* us to understand what we are saying when we engage in moral argument—that they think that, in moral matters, there is safety in obscurity. Undoubtedly there are a lot of people going around in this area who positively prefer obscurity to clarity. But to make this a general accusation would be unfair. There are others who attack modern moral philosophy for a more respectable reason—though not an entirely cogent one. They think, rightly, that there are important moral questions of substance that we have to answer, and that moral philosophers ought to be helping us to answer them. With this we can agree. But then they go on to say that therefore moral philosophers ought to go straight on to the questions of substance, and not get side-tracked into questions about meaning. Their mistake is not to see that the moral philosopher's distinctive contribution to the discussion of the substantive moral questions *is* the investigation of the words and concepts, and thus the logic, that are being employed. If they ask the moral philosopher to leave this conceptual discussion and get on to the substantial issues, they are asking him to stop being a moral philosopher. But I believe that the conceptual discussion *can* contribute to the practical discussion, and that I have shown this in my writings on practical issues. I shall try to placate these opponents of modern moral philosophy by discussing the theoretical issues always in relation to their bearing on practical questions. I hope that we shall end up seeing that theory is relevant to practice.

TAXONOMY OF ETHICAL THEORIES

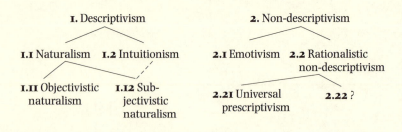

1. Descriptivism: Meanings of moral statements are wholly determined by syntax and truth conditions.
1.1 Naturalism: Truth conditions of moral statements are non-moral properties.
1.11 Objectivistic naturalism: These properties are objective.
1.12 Subjectivistic naturalism: These properties are subjective.
1.2 Intuitionism: Truth conditions of moral statements are *sui generis* moral properties
2. Non-descriptivism: Meanings of moral statements are not wholly determined by syntax and truth conditions.
2.1 Emotivism: Moral statements are not governed by logic.
2.2 Rationalistic non-descriptivism: Moral statements are governed by logic.
2.21 Universal prescriptivism: The logic which governs moral statements is the logic of universal prescriptions.
2.22 ?

REQUIREMENTS FOR AN ADEQUATE ETHICAL THEORY (see pp. 112 ff.)

	Objectivistic naturalism	Subjectivistic naturalism	Intuitionism	Emotivism
1. Neutrality	✗	✓	✓	✓
2. Practicality	✗	✗	✗	✓
3. Incompatibility	✓	✗	✓	✓
4. Logicality	✓	✓	✓	✗
5. Arguability	✗	✗	✗	✗
6. Conciliation	✗	✗	✗	✗

A TAXONOMY OF ETHICAL THEORIES

3

TAXONOMY

3.1. I MUST start by saying how happy I am to be addressing a Swedish audience again on a topic in ethical theory. It is never difficult in Sweden, as it has become in many parts of the world, to find serious philosophers who are able to discuss these questions with clarity and rigour. I am also particularly delighted to be giving lectures dedicated to the memory of Axel Hägerström. He could justly be called the pioneer, in recent times, of ethical non-descriptivism, though in fact views of this sort have a long history (see H 1998*a*). He thus made the most important breakthrough in the subject that there has been in this century. And I am delighted also to be giving these lectures in the home town of Linnaeus, the pioneer of scientific taxonomy.

I must begin, though, by explaining the title of these lectures. This involves saying what I mean by 'Ethical Theory', and what I mean by 'Taxonomy'. The first is the more difficult task, because the expression 'Ethical Theory' has been used, and abused, in so many different ways. I am going to use it a good deal more narrowly than many writers—otherwise it would become a subject that could not be covered in five lectures. I mean by it the study of the moral concepts, that is, of our use of the moral words—if you like, of their meaning in a broad sense, or of what we are doing when we ask moral questions. Since, as I have argued (1.1 f.), an important part, at least, of the meaning of all words, including moral words, is determined by their logical properties, this study of meanings leads inescapably to the study of those logical properties. And that is why the subject has practical importance. For one of the chief things that is demanded of the moral philosopher is that he (or she) should do something to help us discuss moral questions rationally; and this requires obedience to the logical rules governing the concepts. Unless we follow these rules, we shall never be able to argue rationally about moral questions. The prime task of philosophy, since Socrates started the business, is the study of arguments; and the prime task of moral philosophy is the study of moral arguments, to learn how to tell good from bad ones. In this task ethical theory, which reveals the logic of the moral concepts, is an essential tool.

It may help confine the subject within bounds if I go on to say what ethical theory, as I am using the term, is not. Many writers now use the expression 'moral theory'. I am never sure quite what they mean by it; it seems to cover a vast area of indeterminate size, but at least includes the views of the writers on a lot of substantial moral questions, systematized often into a number of moral principles, such as Rawls's 'Principles of Justice'. Thus a moral theory cannot be, as I hope ethical theory will be in my hands, a purely formal discipline dealing only in logical and conceptual studies. Kant was very insistent on this distinction between formal and substantial theses (8.5). I am not for a moment denying the importance of using rational argument to decide on substantial moral principles. That is the ambition of all serious moral philosophers. But there is a prior task: that of finding the rules governing the argument. Without those rules, anything goes.

I shall not in these lectures be doing moral theory in that wide sense, though I have in other places devoted a lot of attention to practical moral issues. Nor shall I be doing anything that could be called 'ontology'. I have argued elsewhere (H 1985a) that an ontological dispute like the supposed dispute between realists and anti-realists, if it is a genuine dispute at all, turns fairly rapidly into a dispute which is not ontological but conceptual, and that there is no way of clearly formulating this supposed dispute about whether there really are moral facts or moral properties *in rerum natura* without translating it into a dispute about how moral words get their meaning. So we are only wasting our time (as Hume might have put it, 'amusing ourselves') if we argue about whether moral facts exist without first raising the conceptual issues on which any solution to that problem has to depend. Even if we were to talk about real moral properties *in rerum natura* (and I cannot forbid people to talk in this way if they want to) we shall be only thereby affirming our subscription to the moral statements or principles that we accept. The question remains of what we are doing when we so subscribe to them.

If we ask what we are doing, we shall have to do some conceptual analysis, and the result of it is likely to be that all forms of descriptivism fail to give an adequate account of the matter; there is an essential prescriptive element in the meaning of moral statements which goes beyond their descriptive meaning (1.7, and see Chapters 4 ff.). If we want to be realists about the prescriptive element, we can if we wish speak of real *prescriptive* properties in actions; but that is simply not illuminating.

I shall be using the expression 'ethical theory', then, in the narrow sense of 'theory about the meaning and logical properties of the moral words'. I have already said why I think that it is a necessary study if we are to distinguish good from bad arguments about moral questions. It is surprising, therefore, how many moral philosophers try to persuade us that we do not need to study ethical theory (e.g. Rawls 1971: 51). One reason why people say this may be the following. They have examined various ethical theories that have been put forward, and have (often after insufficient study) decided that these will not do. They have therefore concluded too hastily that *no* ethical theory is adequate. One of the things I shall be doing in these lectures is to take the various possible ethical theories in turn and say what is wrong with each of them. But I shall also go on, unlike the writers I am speaking of, to say what is *right* about each of them. They all reveal different parts of the truth about morality. Instead of jumping to the conclusion, because all ethical theories you know of have faults, that there is no adequate ethical theory, so you had better give up looking for one, the moral philosopher who is less of a defeatist will go on to try to find a theory which preserves the truths in each of these theories but avoids their errors. And that is what I shall be doing in these lectures. If as a result I get branded as an eclectic, so be it (H 1994*b*).

An important part of the search will be an attempt to make a list of the requirements that an adequate ethical theory has to satisfy. Then we can look at each theory in turn and see which of the requirements it satisfies, and which it fails to satisfy. Thus we may be able to correct and improve them, and end up with a theory that satisfies all the requirements.

3.2. So much, then, for the expression 'Ethical Theory'. What about 'Taxonomy'? This is a good deal easier, because I shall be using the term in much the same way as the botanists. I was interested to see that Hägerström himself published a dialogue called *The Botanist and the Philosopher: On the Necessity of Epistemology*; but since it appeared only in Swedish I have been unable to read it to see whether his view of the relations between the two disciplines was the same as mine. When your great naturalist Linnaeus set out to classify plants, he followed Aristotle in classifying them *per genus et differentiam*. But since his classification had many more than the two levels of genus and species, Linnaeus introduced other words for the intermediate levels: for example, 'family'. I do not think that Aristotle would have quarrelled with this, for he certainly did not want to classify only at two levels. The term 'species' is still in use: each species is distinguished within a genus or subordinate class by stating the difference that marks it out from the other species.

However, I shall perhaps be closer to Aristotle than to Linnaeus in one respect. Linnaeus was doing an empirical study; he had to take the various plants as he found them, and put them into a clear and consistent classification. But in philosophy we can do more than this. Because the enquiry is a formal one, it is legitimate to ask, not just what theories we can find in the world, but what theories we *could* find. This question ought to be answerable a priori. In the case of each division that we make in the course of our taxonomy, we can ask, not merely what species of ethical theory there have been, but what theories there *could* be. So, instead of going to the Amazon jungle to look for new species, we can think them out for ourselves. That is the way the subject progresses.

So what I shall be attempting in these lectures will be very ambitious (perhaps dangerously so). I shall try to show, in the case of each division that I make in the taxonomy, that the division is *exhaustive*. The easiest way of doing this, which for the most part I shall be following, is by making each division a *dichotomy*—that is, a division into just two classes which between them exhaust the genus. This can be achieved by making the *differentia* of each species the negation of the *differentia* of the other. I shall be giving an illustration of this in a moment, when I make the main division of ethical theories into the two genera, descriptivism and non-descriptivism. If it were possible to realize this ambition and make the taxonomy exhaustive, then at the end of the day we should have a complete classification of possible ethical theories, with a demonstration that these were the only possible ones. If it turned out that all the possible ones were inadequate, then we really should have to give up all hope of finding an adequate one. But I am more optimistic.

The main division of ethical theories that I shall make is into two genera, which I shall call 'descriptivism' and 'non-descriptivism'. Our first task, therefore, is to give the *differentia* between these. On this there has been much confusion. Terms like 'realist' and 'anti-realist', 'cognitivist' and 'non-cognitivist', and others have been widely used, as if they all marked the same distinction. In a paper I have already referred to I have argued that the pair of terms 'descriptivist' and 'non-descriptivist' is the clearest way of making the distinction, and that the others, as soon as they are clarified, collapse into it. But the position is worse than that, because, when those who engage in these disputes try to give the *differentia* between their positions, they commonly choose a misleading one, namely whether, according to a given theory, moral statements can be true or false. I shall be arguing in 2.6 that no relevant dispute is marked out by this question, nor by the question of whether we can know them to be true, nor by the question of whether moral facts or moral properties exist in the world. This is because there are perfectly good senses in which a non-descriptivist like me can allow that moral statements can be true or false, that we can know some of them to be true, and that there are moral properties (H 1976*b*, 1985*a*, 1995*b*). If I demur to the claim that there are moral facts in the world, it is because I do not like saying that there are *any* facts in the world. The world consists of things, not facts. But that is another story (H 1985*a*).

3.3. First, let me give you *my* way of distinguishing descriptivism from non-descriptivism; and then I will tell you why I think other ways lead to confusions. My *differentia* relies on the notion of truth conditions—but not in the simple way that some people might think. It is commonly thought that meaning depends in some way on truth conditions (H 1991*a*, 1993*g*, 1995*b*). This was the basis of the old veri-fication theory of meaning which many logical positivists embraced, but which is now in disrepute in its early simple form which claimed that 'the meaning of a sentence is the method of its verification'. However, it is even now common to claim that truth conditions have a part to play in determining meaning; and I agree with this. 'Meaning' has here to be understood as including both sense and ref-erence. This was how Austin used it (1962: 100). To be accurate, I must also explain that I am thinking here of the meaning of a token sentence as used by a particular speaker on a particular occasion. We might make a first approximation to explaining what descriptivism is by saying that it is the view that meaning is *wholly* determined by truth conditions. If this is held to be true of the meaning of all sen-tences, then that is descriptivism *tout court*. There have perhaps been people who have thought this, the victims of what Austin called 'the descriptive fallacy' (1961: 234; 1962: 3). I shall not say anything about this very sweeping view. Ethical descriptivism, as a first approxima-tion, is the view that the meaning of a moral statement is wholly de-termined by its truth-conditions, that is, by the conditions under which it would correctly be said to be true.

On this view, moral statements get their meaning in just the same way as ordinary factual statements. But we have to ask whether even in the case of ordinary factual statements it is true that they get their meaning *wholly* from their truth-conditions. The answer seems to be that they do not. It has been common, when discussing meaning, to distinguish between semantics and syntactics. I will leave the third member or supposed member of this triad, 'pragmatics', till much later (6.5). The distinction has been made in various and often inconsistent ways; but I shall use 'semantics' not, as some do, widely to cover anything to do with meaning, but narrowly to include *only* that part of the meaning of sentences which is determined directly or indirectly by truth conditions. This leaves, as another constituent of meaning, the syntactical properties of sentences. For example, if a statement is of the subject–predicate form, that partly determines its meaning; and we can know this before we know what its truth conditions are.

Not all grammatical distinctions are relevant to meaning. For example, as we have seen, the distinction between strong and weak verbs is not (1.3). If I say 'the sun shined' instead of 'the sun shone', I speak ungrammatically but my meaning is still clear, and the same. But some are relevant. The clearest example is the distinction between the indicative and imperative verb-forms (1.3, H 1996*b*). The transformation which changes the Latin '*ibis*', meaning 'You will (or are going to) go', into the imperative '*i*', meaning 'Go', alters the meaning. Sometimes the grammatical or syntactical properties affect the logical properties. To take the same example, there is a valid inference from the future indicative 'You will go' to the future indicative 'You will not stay here', but not from the imperative 'Go' to the indicative 'You will not stay here'. Some commands are not obeyed.

Confining ourselves, therefore, to syntactical or grammatical properties which do affect meaning, we can say that they are a part of the meaning-determining properties of sentences which are independent of any particular truth conditions. So it is not true, on any at all plausible theory, that all meaning is determined by truth conditions. So our proposed *differentia*, which said that according to descriptivism the meaning of moral sentences is entirely determined by the truth conditions of statements expressed by them, has to be refined.

The position is rather this. The syntactical or formal properties of a sentence (those of them that affect meaning) determine what kind of sentence it is. They do this by determining its internal structure. For example, they may make it into a subject–predicate sentence, apt for ascribing a property to an object. *What* property to *what* object, they do not determine. That is the role of the sentence's semantics, not of its syntactics.

Truth conditions belong to semantics. That a statement has to have truth conditions is determined when it has been specified that it is a statement. Statements are speech acts which can be true or false. If a putative statement has no truth conditions, it is no genuine statement. This does not stop it being a meaningful speech act; for there are many kinds of meaningful speech act which do not have truth conditions, because they just cannot be true or false. Imperative speech acts (or imperations as we have called them) are an example.

Austin and his disciples have distinguished between meaning and illocutionary force. William Alston, by contrast, has included in the meaningful elements in sentences what he calls 'illocutionary force indicating devices' (1964: 37 ff.); see also Searle 1969: 62 and Searle and Vanderveken 1985: 7. I have called these in 1.3, H 1989*a* tropics. I think Alston and Searle are right to say that there is a wide sense of 'meaning' in which these contribute to the meaning of sentences. An example is the feature which distinguishes imperative from indicative sentences, such as exists in most languages. I am inclined to doubt whether Austin himself would have dissented from this (see H 1971*c*: 100 ff.); but some of his disciples seem to.

It can readily be admitted that sentences of the same form and content can sometimes be used to perform different speech acts with different illocutionary forces. For example 'You will go' could express a prediction, but it could (at least in the British Army) express a command. But this may be like any other ambiguity. Just as 'I will meet you at the bank' could be referring to the river bank or the place where you get money, so, equally, the word 'will' could be the sign of a prediction, or of a promise (two different kinds of speech act). All we need say is that somebody who took the sentence in a way different from that in which the speaker intended it would have misunderstood his meaning; the speaker was intending to perform one kind of speech act, but the hearer took him to be performing a different kind.

There are plenty of other examples in the literature, but none of them has convinced me that illocutionary force is not part of meaning.

'I warn you' is sometimes used as a supposed example of the impossibility of distinguishing illocutionary from perlocutionary acts. But this too is ambiguous. Road hazard signs used to be followed by a sign saying 'You have been warned'. Now they are sometimes followed by a sign saying 'Be warned'. There must be two different senses of 'warn' here, because one can hardly be instructed to be warned if one has already been warned. In one sense 'warn' means 'address a warning to'. But in another sense it means 'put on one's guard by means of a warning'. 'Be warned' uses the latter sense, in which the speech act is not successful unless the perlocutionary act has been effective; but 'You have been warned' simply reports the performance of an illocutionary act, whether or not the addressee has actually been put on his guard.

3.4. If the syntactical or grammatical properties of sentences include their illocutionary force indicating devices (of which mood-signs are an example), then we can restate our *differentia* in a clearer way. A descriptivist is someone who thinks, not merely that a moral statement has truth conditions (for non-descriptivists can agree to this, as we shall see); nor that a moral statement's meaning is wholly determined by its truth conditions (for, as we have seen, this is not true of any sentences); nor that the syntactical or grammatical properties of sentences expressing moral statements make their illocutionary forces such that they have to have truth conditions, and are therefore statements in the sense just used (this too the non-descriptivist can agree to); but further, that these truth conditions are all that is needed in addition to determine the meaning of the sentences. A non-descriptivist, then, will be someone who denies this last clause; he thinks that moral statements, although they may have truth conditions, do not depend for their meaning wholly on those truth conditions, nor even wholly on their syntactical features plus their truth conditions, because their syntactical features allow them to be used with the same meaning, although the truth conditions may vary (7.3, H 1993*g*, 1995*b*).

This is a difficult idea to grasp, so I must try to explain it more simply. I can do so by using a term first introduced, so far as I know, by Stevenson (1945: 62). He distinguished between the descriptive meaning of moral statements and their emotive meaning. I shall later be discarding the idea of emotive meaning; I shall substitute for it the term 'evaluative meaning' (see *LM* ch. 7). Sometimes I shall say 'prescriptive meaning', but the difference between these two expressions need not now concern us. This will enable me to leave behind the 'pragmatics' which play such a large part in Stevenson's theory, and which I think are flawed (1.5, 6.5, H 1996*b*). So I shall distinguish between the descriptive and the evaluative meaning of moral statements. The descriptive meaning is really the same thing as the truth conditions, plus the requirement, laid on a moral statement by its having the illocutionary force of a statement, that it has to have truth conditions in order to have meaning (H 1993*g*). The descriptive meaning is also the same thing as the semantics of the statement. It determines to what the descriptive terms in the statement can correctly be applied, and to what objects the referring expressions used in it must be taken as referring. Thus the descriptive meaning does uniquely determine the truth conditions of the statement.

But—and here is the important point for our *differentia* between descriptivists and non-descriptivists—*both* the truth conditions *and* the descriptive meaning of a moral statement can vary, without the meaning of the statement varying totally. This is because the evaluative meaning, the other constituent in the meaning, can remain the same. In other words, the crucial *differentia* between a descriptivist and a non-descriptivist is this: the descriptivist thinks that if the truth conditions of a moral statement have changed, its meaning as a whole must have changed; but a non-descriptivist holds that this is not so. He thinks it possible for a moral statement to retain the same evaluative meaning, while changing its descriptive meaning, and its truth conditions and its semantics. This is because there is an extra bit of input that goes into the making of a moral statement which is not present in the making of an ordinary purely descriptive statement.

An example may make this clearer. Suppose that I have called a woman a good person, thus making a moral statement about her. I have made this statement because the person has certain descriptive qualities; *they* were, for me, the truth conditions of the statement that I made. That is, if the person had not had these features, I would not have made the statement, and if she had them, my existing moral standards required me to make it. So, according to my existing standards, having the features was both a necessary and a sufficient condition for making the statement. The features might be partly positive and partly negative: they might have included, for example, that she is kind and generous, and does not cheat at cards. If she cheated, I would not call her a good person, and if she were not kind and generous I would not either. And of course we have to add to these qualities all the other positive and negative qualities she has to have or lack, and these may include disjunctions of alternative qualities.

But now suppose that my standards change. Perhaps I have become more hard-bitten, and now think it is all right to cheat at cards and that kindness and generosity are a sign of weak-mindedness. I shall now say that she is not a good person just because of the very same properties that made me call her a good person before. So am I still using the phrase 'good person' with the same meaning as before, or am I not? I want to say that in one sense I am, and in another I am not. I am still using it with the same evaluative meaning: to call someone a good person is still to commend her (or him). It follows that I have *changed my mind*. What I am now saying contradicts what I was saying before. It is therefore impossible for anybody consistently to agree both with what I am saying now and with what I was saying before. To say that both are right would be to commit a logical error. This would not be so if the meaning of my words had entirely changed; for then what I am now saying would not be the negation of what I then said. But I am using the words now with a different descriptive meaning—that is, in accordance with different standards, or different truth conditions. Examples like this show quite clearly that there are these two elements in the meanings of evaluative expressions like 'good'. Only philosophers with axes to grind deny this.

It will be noticed that in giving the descriptive meaning or truth conditions of the expression 'good person' in my example I used the words 'kind' and 'generous' and 'cheat'. In case anyone wants to object that these too are evaluative expressions, so that the statement of the truth conditions is itself not *wholly* descriptive, I must say that these words too, which belong to a class of what I shall call 'secondarily evaluative words', and which others have called 'thick ethical concepts', can be treated in a similar way to 'good', except that their evaluative meaning is secondary to their descriptive; but that will have to be left till later (3.8, H 1996*d*).

3.5. The important point I wish to make now is that, although evaluative (including moral) statements do indeed have truth conditions, these can change without the entire meaning of the sentences which express them changing (H 1993*g*, 1996*e*). This has crucial consequences for ethical theory. If we change the truth conditions of a moral statement, we change its descriptive meaning. But if the evaluative meaning remains the same, we have, in making this change, altered our moral standards. We are appealing to different reasons, for example, for calling an act wrong, but we are calling it wrong in the same sense, evaluatively speaking. We are still condemning it by calling it wrong.

This means that a statement of the truth conditions of moral statements, which may signal a change in moral standards, is not itself morally neutral. So there can be no question of there being a first stage in the construction of an ethical theory in which we give a morally neutral general formulation of the truth conditions of moral statements, and then a second stage in which we use this general formulation to determine which moral statements in particular are true. In the general formulation, we will already have sold the pass by making some substantial moral claims—which is what you are always doing when you are giving the truth conditions of moral statements. In other and simpler words, it is no use thinking that the standards by which we assess the truth of moral statements are morally neutral. They are the very same standards as those by which we make the moral statements themselves, and so incorporate a substantial moral stance. In our example, if you say that cheating at cards does not make a person a bad person, you are making a substantial moral claim.

I said earlier that a descriptivist is someone who thinks that, apart

from their syntactical features (which may determine their illocutionary force among other things), the only additional determinant
of meaning for moral statements is their truth conditions. This is
what the non-descriptivist denies. He thinks, on the contrary, that
there is another element in the meaning of these statements, the
evaluative or prescriptive, which can remain the same although the
truth conditions change, and which make it the same statement, in
the sense that it still makes the same evaluation of the same act, person, etc., although its truth conditions have changed. This is a thing
that could never happen with ordinary descriptive or factual statements. In their case, if the truth conditions change, it is altogether a
different statement. With moral statements, by contrast, 'She is a
good person' can be affirmed by one speaker but denied by another
because they use different standards and different truth conditions,
and yet be, in respect of its evaluative meaning, the same statement.
This too has important consequences, as we shall see when I come to
discuss subjectivism (5.5); it means that these two speakers really are
contradicting one another, which would not be the case on a subjectivist theory which held that they were just making statements about
their own respective attitudes of approval and disapproval, and would
also not be the case, as we shall see, on an objectivistic naturalist
theory which held that different moral standards entail different
meanings for the moral words (4.3).

It is clear from these explanations (which I fear have been complicated and hard to grasp—which is why so few people grasp them)
that my main division between descriptivist and non-descriptivist ethical theories is an exhaustive division. The first kind of theory, as I
have just said, affirms what the second denies, namely, that apart
from their syntactical features, the only additional determinant of
meaning for moral statements is their truth conditions. I hope that by
differentiating the genera in this dichotomous way I have made it the
case that there cannot be a theory which falls into neither of the two
genera. So if, as I hope to do, I can show that descriptivism, in all its
different forms, is inadequate, I shall thereby have shown that one
has to be some kind of non-descriptivist. After rejecting an untenable
kind, I shall advocate a kind which I think is more tenable; but I shall

leave it open whether there may also be other kinds that are tenable too.

3.6. I hope that what I have said has shown how little grasp of these issues those people have who think (as many beginner students are taught to think) that it is sufficient to distinguish between what they call cognitivist and non-cognitivist ethical theories by saying that they give opposing answers to the question 'Can moral statements be true or false?' The answer to this question is that they can, but that the important issue between descriptivists and non-descriptivists is not settled thereby (H 1995*b*, 1996*e*).

The terms 'cognitivist' and 'non-cognitivist' are misleading for a further reason. The etymology of these words seems to imply that according to cognitivists one can *know* that a moral statement is true, but according to non-cognitivists one cannot. This is quite misleading. The important question is whether one can *think rationally* about moral questions. In other words, are there ways of doing our moral reasoning well or badly? This important question is concealed by those who speak of cognitivism and non-cognitivism, and of knowing that moral statements are true.

I can perhaps show this by taking the word 'know' and doing the same with it as I have just been doing with the word 'true'. You remember my example of someone who said that a person was a good person, and said this because, among other things, the person was kind and generous and never cheated at cards. I am sure that this speaker would claim that what he said was true, and that he knew that it was true. The linguistic phenomena are not in doubt. He knew, that is, that the person *was* kind and generous and never cheated. And this made his statement true according to the standards or truth conditions that he was using. As to the standards, he had no doubt learnt these standards and not forgotten them. He *knew* that people who are kind and generous can be called, so far as that goes, good people, and that people who cheat at cards cannot be called good people. If anybody does not know this, he would say, his education has been neglected. But the more hard-bitten person who contradicted him in the example could not, all the same, be ruled out of court. The two disagree about the standards to be used in assessing the goodness of people. And both may say that they know that their respective standards are the right ones. And about the word 'right' as used in these claims, all the same things can be said as I have said about the word 'true' (H 1976*b*, 1991*a*). So nothing is gained by introducing the word 'know' into this discussion; and it is misleading because it suggests that what is known cannot be disputed; but it *will be* disputed.

The important question, I said, was whether there are good and bad ways of reasoning about *all* these matters: about whether the standards and truth conditions that are being used are the ones that ought to be being used, and so about which of the statements made by our two opposing parties we ought, at the end of the day, to call true. This comes to the same as asking how we can rightly reason about what our moral principles concerning kindness and generosity and cheating at cards are to be (H 1993*g*). That question is just waved aside by those who speak in the way I have been complaining of. We shall return to it (7.8).

3.7. Before I end this part of the discussion I want to say a bit more about the word 'true'. Up to now I have spoken as if it meant no more than 'satisfying the truth conditions, whatever those are'. But the word 'true' has also certain formal properties which we must not ignore. In giving an account of these, I am much indebted to Crispin Wright (1992). An example of these formal properties is the Tarskian thesis that if *p*, then it is true that *p*, and vice versa. I suppose that some opponent of mine might seek to controvert what I have been saying by claiming that these formal properties block the road to a non-descriptivist account of moral statements, or at least to the non-descriptivist's right to use 'true' of them. But they do not.

To explain this, I have to say something about the *endorsing* function of the word 'true', which was first, I think, brought into the open by Strawson a long time ago (1949, 1950). Though we do not say all that can be said about the word 'true' in saying that it is a word we use for endorsing what someone has said, it does have this function; and this function is by itself enough to account for the Tarski phenomenon. There are some differences between the words 'true' and 'right', both of which are used for endorsing; but these I have discussed elsewhere (H 1976*b*).

If I say that *p* (some statement) is true, I thereby endorse it. But it is obvious that if I say that *p*, I cannot then, in the same breath, refuse to endorse the statement that *p* (the statement that I have just made). This is not merely a matter of pragmatic inconsistency, like that of the statement '*p* but I don't believe that *p*'. If I said '*p*, but it is not true that *p*', I should be actually contradicting myself (H 1995*a*: ii. 272). Similarly, if I endorse the statement that *p*, but refuse to affirm the same statement, I contradict myself. And this is so, even though all the things I said earlier about the variability of the truth conditions of moral statements still hold. A statement has, indeed (like some other speech acts besides statements), to have the formal property that it is something which one can endorse, and which, if one can endorse it, one has, on pain of self-contradiction, to be prepared to make. But this could be so, even though different people might be using different standards or truth conditions when making this kind of statement.

We can admit that in *this* respect (namely the Tarski phenomenon) moral statements behave just like any other kind of statement; but we could go on to say that they differ in other respects. In particular, they differ in that the truth conditions being used by one speaker may differ from those being used by another, *without* the meanings of the two moral statements made by them differing in all respects. If I say of someone 'She is a good person', and someone else says 'No, she is not', then we are contradicting one another, even though we are using different truth conditions; and this is because our evaluations, conveyed by the evaluative meanings of our two utterances, are logically inconsistent with one another. He is refusing to endorse what I have said. So he could have said 'No, that is not true'. All such phenomena will survive my claim that truth conditions can vary without the entire meaning varying. Moral statements will still be, in Crispin Wright's term, 'minimally truth-apt' (1992: 141 ff.).

We may contrast this with what happens with ordinary purely descriptive statements, whose truth conditions cannot vary without *the meaning* of the sentences that express them changing (that is, without their becoming different statements). If I say 'The sky is blue' and someone else says 'No, the sky is not blue', then we are indeed contradicting each other; but it must be the case either that we are disagreeing about the descriptive state of the sky, or that we are using the word 'blue', or one of the other words in the sentences, in different senses. We cannot consistently agree about the descriptive state of the sky *and* use the words in the same senses and still contradict each other. That is, if we agree about the descriptive state of the sky, and agree in our use of the words, there is nothing left for us to disagree about. But in the 'good person' case it might be that we agreed exactly about how the person behaved (what she did), *and* about the (evaluative) meaning of 'good', but were contradicting one another because we were evaluating differently people who did that, or behaved like that. By 'behaved like that' I mean that, for example, they were kind and generous, and did not cheat at cards. And by that I mean that they, for example, gave much of their money to relieve distress and did not hide cards in their sleeves in order to win the game.

These differences between the two kinds of speech act are readily explained by the fact that moral statements have an element in their meaning which purely descriptive utterances like 'The sky is blue' do not have. This is the evaluative element. Purely descriptive utterances have (1) the syntactical element, which in turn determines (2) their illocutionary force (that they are descriptive statements), which in turn requires (3) that they have truth conditions; and they have (4) these particular truth conditions. Evaluative statements, by contrast, have an additional element. They have, as before, (1) the syntactical element, which in turn determines (2) their illocutionary force (that they are evaluative statements), which in turn requires (3) that they have truth conditions; and they have (4) these particular truth conditions; but in addition the illocutionary force requires (5) that they be evaluations; and this in turn means that they can go on having this evaluative illocutionary force even if the truth conditions change. That is how describing is different from evaluating (for example commending). Since evaluating is always according to standards, there will always *be* truth conditions; but the meaning is not exhausted by the truth conditions, and so what remains of the meaning (the evaluative element) is enough to bring about a contradiction between the two parties even though they are using the words with different descriptive meanings. This is the extra bit of input that I mentioned earlier. One of the parties is commending the person and the other is refusing to assent to the commendation. Thus their statements are mutually inconsistent. As Stevenson would have put it, there is a disagreement in attitude which survives the agreement in belief.

3.8. People who disagree with my analysis of evaluative sentences often say that it is not possible in all cases to disentangle the evaluative from the descriptive element in their meanings. But this is wishful thinking on their part. I have been in many discussions of this topic, and in them these descriptivists have often brought up examples in which they say this disentangling is impossible. But I have always been able to achieve it fairly easily.

Here is an example to be going on with. A descriptivist may say that we cannot disentangle the evaluative from the descriptive elements in the meaning of the word 'kind'. But this is really not very difficult. Certainly to call somebody kind is normally to commend him (or her). It is to commend him according to a certain standard. The truth conditions of statements containing the word are fairly well known, although admittedly not precise. Suppose now that someone gives much of his money to relieve distress. Nearly all of us would say that such a person was kind. But there might be someone who thought that it was not a characteristic of a good person to do this. This person could agree that someone did this (namely gave much of his money to relieve distress), but might *condemn* his doing this. He would then not be able to use 'kind' as a term of commendation. But he might well be able to recognize the sort of people that the others called kind. So he would know well the descriptive meaning they attached to the word. But he would not use it, because it carried an evaluative meaning to which he could not subscribe. He might stop using the word altogether (*FR* 10.1 n.), or he might use it 'in inverted commas', to signify that a person had the descriptive qualities expected by most people in those called kind; he would be able to use the word 'kind' purely descriptively, to signify the possession of those commonly esteemed qualities, without himself esteeming them (*LM* 7.5, *FR* 10.2).

I am quite confident that the same treatment could be given to any example of a 'thick' or secondarily evaluative concept that was alleged to have descriptive and evaluative meanings that cannot be disentangled. On this, see Millgram's comments (1995) on Williams (1985: 140 ff.). One particular argument of those who claim this should perhaps be mentioned. It is often said that if we had just the descriptive meaning of 'kind' we might, indeed, be able to recognize examples of kind people in the existing descriptive sense of the word, but would be unable to extend or extrapolate its use to new and perhaps slightly different examples. This seems to me to be simply false. Suppose that I am the hard-bitten person I mentioned earlier, and can recognize the qualities that people call kind and esteem, but do not myself esteem them. And suppose that some new example is produced of a person who does not have *exactly* those qualities, but has qualities very like them, so that people who *do* esteem them are likely to esteem that person too, and call him kind. I can see no difficulty in my predicting that this is what they will do. In order to make this prediction I do not myself have to esteem the qualities or the person; I only have to be confident that *they* will. I find it surprising that people should rely on this very weak argument.

I have elsewhere (H 1986*c* = 1989: 116 ff.) gone into a lot of detail about the behaviour of these secondarily evaluative or thick concepts; so I do not need to do it again now. The motives of those who make such play with these concepts are fairly easy to divine. They were not actually the first to discover the distinction between thick and thin concepts: see *LM* 7.5, *FR* 2.7. But they found them attractive because they *seem* to impugn the distinction between descriptive and evaluative expressions. Their useful feature, for descriptivist arguments, is that they have a descriptive meaning which is fairly securely attached to them. If one does not recognize as kind the sort of actions that kind people do, then one might be said not to know the meaning of the word. Yet they are also, in their normal use, undeniably evaluative, in that someone who called a person kind would be taken by nearly everyone to be commending him. So it is easy to see why de-scriptivists latched on to these words in the hope of casting doubt on non-descriptivist theories. But a little more attention to the analysis of these concepts would have shown them, if they were willing to be shown, how the two elements in the meaning of these words are re-lated and how they can be distinguished.

4

NATURALISM

4.1. In the preceding chapter I made the main division of ethical theories into two genera, which I called descriptivist and non-descriptivist theories. I said that the *differentia* between these was that descriptivist theories affirm, but that non-descriptivist theories deny, that, apart from syntactical features, the meanings of moral statements are determined entirely by their truth conditions. In this and the next chapter I am going to look at the different possible kinds of descriptivist theories. I shall divide these up in the first place according to the *kind* of truth conditions that they say determine the meanings of moral statements. The first division to be made is into those theories which hold that the truth conditions are the possession, by the actions, people, etc. about which the moral statements are made, of what I shall call, following tradition, *natural* properties. This is not an entirely helpful term, and I shall have to explain it. But, again following tradition, I shall call theories that use this kind of truth condition in giving the meanings of moral statements *naturalist* theories (H 1996*d*).

I shall contrast them with theories which hold that the truth conditions which determine the meanings of moral statements are the possession by actions, people, etc. of specifically moral (sometimes classified as 'non-natural') properties. They are sometimes called '*sui generis*' properties. I shall call such theories (still following tradition) *intuitionist* theories. This term too is unhelpful unless explained, and has been used in different ways, especially recently. I might have used instead the expression 'non-naturalist theories', and this would have had the advantage of making explicit the dichotomous nature of my classification. But I avoid it, because a non-naturalist theory might be taken to mean *any* theory that rejected naturalism; and this would be misleading, because all non-descriptivist theories too reject naturalism along with descriptivist theories in general. I am in this sense a non-naturalist: I reject naturalism. But if I called myself a non-naturalist I might be thought to be allying myself with the intuitionists, that is, with the kind of *descriptivists* who reject naturalism (such as Moore and Prichard). I do not want to give this impression. So at least, instead of 'non-naturalist', I should have to say 'non-natural descriptivist', and that would be intolerably cumbrous. So I ask you to pardon me if I go on using the term 'intuitionist', in spite of its ambiguity. What I mean by it will become clear in due course.

However, it does seem possible to divide descriptivist ethical theories in this way by looking at the different kinds of properties which they say have to go into a formulation of the truth conditions of moral statements. Moore had so much difficulty in saying what he meant by 'non-natural property' that in the end he gave up the term. Perhaps there *are* no such properties. But an intuitionist, at any rate, has to think that there are these *sui generis* properties like goodness and wrongness which people, actions, etc. can have. The only definition that can be given of them is negative: we can say that a naturalist is someone who thinks that the truth conditions of moral statements require the possession by their subjects of properties which can be defined, or their meaning explained, without using any specifically moral terms, but that an intuitionist is someone who thinks that in order to give the truth conditions of these statements we have to use specifically moral terms. There would be nothing very scandalous in this. Philosophers continue to argue about whether *modal* terms like 'possible' and 'necessary' can be defined without using other modal terms in the definition. In both the moral and the modal cases the issue is whether we can ever break out of the circle. This resemblance is no accident, because the affinity between moral and modal terms is very strong, as is shown by the existence of the subject called 'deontic logic'. Deontic modalities like 'ought' have a lot in common with logical, alethic, or causal modalities like 'necessary'; and the different sorts of modal logic which deal with these kinds of modality therefore bear a striking resemblance to each other. It would not be extraordinary if in all these cases there were a circle out of which we could not break (H 1996*d*: 354). I shall not, however, now digress into the subject of modalities. Let me simply say that we can make a dichotomous division of descriptivist theories into those, the naturalist ones, which say that the truth conditions of moral statements can be specified without using any moral terms, and those, the intuitionist ones, which say that they cannot. I shall now try to show that both these kinds of descriptivism, the naturalist kind and the intuitionist kind, get into trouble, and that the trouble is the same in both cases. The trouble is that they both collapse into relativism (H 1986c, 1993g). This term too I shall have to explain. Since the main purpose of most of those who embrace descriptivism is to *avoid* relativism, this is a surprising result, and shows that something has gone seriously wrong. What it is, we shall shortly discover.

I have put the distinction between naturalism and intuitionism in terms of the different kinds of truth-conditions they impose on moral statements. My distinction is therefore broad enough to cover both the old-style 'refutation of naturalism' due to Moore (1903), and the new-style naturalism whose chief habitat is Cornell. The old and the new naturalisms are not so different as is commonly supposed; Horgan and Timmons (1992) have adapted Moore's open question argument to refute the new naturalism (H 1996d). But the way I have put the distinction will make it apply to both the old and the new naturalisms. I discuss in the same paper the whole question of whether, as Pigden (1991) appears to think, the fashionable new metaphysics of Putnam and others can help the naturalists; and this must be my excuse for not venturing on it here.

4.2. Let us then look first at naturalist theories. They can in turn be subdivided. Given that they have to specify the truth conditions of moral statements without using any moral terms, they still have a choice as to the kind of terms they *will* use in specifying the truth conditions. Some kinds of naturalist specify the truth conditions without reference to the attitudes, etc. of the speakers of the statements, or of their society. I am going to call this kind of naturalist an *objectivist* naturalist. Other kinds of naturalist specify the truth conditions of moral statements in terms of the attitudes, etc. of the people who make them. I shall call such people *subjectivist* naturalists. I am going to deal now with objectivist naturalism, and come back to subjectivist naturalism later, after I have dealt with intuitionism. The reason for this postponement is that there are very strong resemblances between intuitionism and subjectivist naturalism, although these resemblances are usually ignored or repudiated by intuitionists. And for short I shall in what follows call objectivist naturalism simply 'naturalism'. It is by far the most important variety of naturalism, and exhibits very clearly the dangers of this kind of theory.

The truth conditions of moral statements are determined by the correct application of moral predicates like 'right', 'wrong', 'good', and 'bad' to actions or people. This is true on all theories, both descriptivist and, as we shall later see, non-descriptivist (7.8, H 1995*b*). Suppose, therefore, that we were to try to find out what these truth conditions are by discovering to what actions or people these predicates are correctly applied. If our enquiry were successful, we should then have established *the* truth conditions of the statements. But how do we discover to what objects predicates are correctly applied? In the case of predicates in general, we do it by examining the linguistic usage of native speakers of the language; and I can see no reason for thinking (at least no reason why a naturalist should think) that it is any different with *moral* predicates. Indeed, this seems to be the only way a naturalist *could* determine their use in common parlance. Suppose, therefore, that, taking 'wrong' as an example, we examine the use of this predicate by native speakers of English (one could do the same in Swedish, but I will not try, because to my regret I do not speak it). We shall discover that native speakers of English apply the predicate 'wrong' to certain sorts of actions, and refuse to apply it to other sorts. Can we therefore say that the truth conditions of statements containing the predicate 'wrong' (in its moral use) are these: the statements are true if in them the predicate 'wrong' is applied to the sorts of actions to which native speakers of English do apply them, and false if in them the predicate 'wrong' is applied to the sorts of actions to which native speakers of English do not apply them?

But there is a snag here which we must be careful to avoid. What do we mean by 'the sorts of actions'? In order for this piece of linguistic research to give an objective result, we shall have to be able to recognize and specify the sorts of actions that the words are being

applied to *without* appealing to anything except the observable linguistic behaviour of the speakers and the observable properties of the
actions. If we were to appeal, for example, to *our own* assessment of
the actions as right or wrong, that would vitiate the research. For if
we did this, then what we should discover is not what actions in particular the speakers were applying the words to, but rather whether
their assessment of the actions corresponded to our own. We need to
be able to specify the sorts of actions to which they apply the words in
a morally neutral way; otherwise we shall not be doing the research
in the way that a truly naturalistic theory has to. We have to establish
that these are the (neutrally specified) sorts of actions to which the
words are applied by native speakers.

If this is the way our research goes, we shall have achieved *something*. We shall have discovered a rule for the application of the predicate 'wrong' such that, if we follow it, we shall conform perfectly to
the usage, as regards the application of this word, of those whose
usage we were studying, that is, of native speakers of English. And
this is indeed what we could quite safely do with ordinary descriptive
predicates. If we wanted to find a rule for the correct application of
the English word 'red', for example, and thus find out the truth conditions of statements containing it, we could safely do it by seeing to
what sorts of things native speakers of English applied this adjective.
If we then applied it to those and only those sorts of things, we should
be applying it correctly, and our statements would be true.

But if we try to follow this procedure with the word 'wrong', we
shall at once get into difficulties. Not all native speakers of English
apply the predicate 'wrong' to the same sorts of things, not even in
England, let alone in America or Australia. Perhaps, if I had been
doing this in Swedish, I should not have got into so much trouble,
because Sweden has a fairly homogeneous moral culture, and it
might be, though I rather doubt it, that all native speakers of Swedish
apply the word 'wrong' to the very same sorts of things. But even in
Sweden, can it be the case that there are no instances of divergence
in the use of the Swedish word for 'wrong'? I am sure that in fact it is
not the case. Suppose we are talking about eating non-human ani-
mals. I am quite sure that I shall find many Swedes who say that this

is not wrong, but some who say that it *is* wrong. With English this is even more obvious. There are a great many kinds of thing which *some* English speakers call wrong but others do not. Think, for example, of abortion, or of fighting in wars (2.2, 6.9). So we shall not find a single rule for the correct application of the word (a set of truth conditions for statements containing it) which will do for us what the rule for the use of 'red' did. We shall not find a rule, that is, by conforming to which we can be sure of making true moral statements. Rather, we shall find a great many rules, inconsistent with one another, and shall simply not know, by this method, how to use the word.

I want to ask, what is the status of these conflicting rules for the use of 'wrong'? Following the naturalists, we have been assuming that what we were discovering was a rule for the correct application of the word, and nothing more. But we now see that that was not what we were discovering. At least, if we were discovering a rule for the correct application of the word, it was not a purely linguistic rule. It was in fact a substantial moral rule (1996*d*). If one lot of people say that abortion is wrong and another lot say it is not wrong, they are not differing merely in their linguistic usage. They are expressing different moral opinions. This shows very clearly what is wrong with naturalism. What is wrong is that it pretends that what are in fact substantial moral principles are nothing more than linguistic rules. Naturalism confuses learning morals with learning a language. But the two are very different. If I have grown up thinking that abortion is wrong, I have acquired more than a mere linguistic skill. I have acquired a moral principle, an attitude to abortion.

4.3. Now I think you will be able to see why the naturalist kind of descriptivism leads inevitably to relativism (H 1993*g*). There are in most languages words which we translate 'wrong'. These words are, as they are used, rough equivalents to one another. But the cultures that use these words call quite different things wrong. In one culture, for example, it may be thought wrong not to fight for one's country, in another more pacific culture it may be thought wrong to fight. The important thing to get hold of is that, although the people in these cultures hold different opinions about the wrongness of fighting, they may be using the word 'wrong', or its equivalents, in the same sense.

Otherwise they would not be contradicting one another, which they clearly are. The people in one culture are saying that fighting is wrong, and the people in the other are saying that it is not wrong, *in the same sense of 'wrong'*, so far as its evaluative meaning goes (cf. *LM* 6.6, *FR* 6.5, *MT* 4.2). But if we follow the naturalists, we shall have to say that the senses of the word in the two cultures are entirely different. This will have the consequence that they are not contradicting one another; for fighting might be wrong in the sense of the word used by one culture, but not wrong in the sense of the word used by the other. The people in each culture will be right in their own sense of the word 'wrong'. If we distinguish the senses by using different subscripts, we can say that one of the cultures thinks fighting is wrong$_1$, but that the other thinks it is not wrong$_2$. But these two opinions may be mutually consistent, if the two senses of 'wrong' are different.

There would be no harm in this if all they were doing were *describing* the act of fighting. They would just be attributing various descriptive properties to the act of fighting. The trouble starts when we begin using 'wrong' for the purpose for which it actually *is* used in language, namely for *condemning* acts. The naturalist, in accordance with his descriptivism, cannot include this purpose in his account of the meaning of 'wrong'. But it is very natural, since this *is* actually its use, to think that the people in the two cultures are, respectively, condemning and refusing to condemn the act of fighting. Then they *are* contradicting each other. But according to the naturalist they may both be right in what they say. There is no contradiction. The naturalist seems to be led to the conclusion that it is both right for one culture to condemn fighting, and right for the other culture not to condemn it. And this is a relativist position. I shall answer below (4.6) the objection that the example of attitudes to fighting is unfair, as not sufficiently 'basic', and that we should have taken as an example attitudes to 'human flourishing'.

But first we must examine a possible escape route for the naturalist from what we have said so far. The naturalist might seek to escape this conclusion by saying (as in consistency with his position he must) that in calling acts wrong one is *not* condemning them. He is in fact in a dilemma. Either he says that to call an act wrong is to condemn it, in which case his theory lands him in relativism. Or he says that to call an act wrong is not to condemn it, in which case it is very hard to say what he thinks 'wrong' does mean. And even if he says this, he is involved in a kind of relativism; for he is left saying that people who call the act of fighting wrong and people who call it not wrong are both right. They *could* both be right if the word means different things in the two cultures. But this too is a kind of relativism. At any rate, he is likely to be left in the position embraced by Professor MacIntyre (1984), that people in different cultures simply cannot communicate with one another, because they lack the linguistic means of doing so. But since I have written at length about MacIntyre's position elsewhere (H 1986c), I will not say anything about it now.

4.4. People who incline to naturalism sometimes say that in arguments like the one I have just been setting out it is simply *assumed* that a distinction can be made between evaluative and descriptive words, but that in fact no such distinction can be drawn: the words we call 'evaluative' are simply one kind of descriptive word. We may reply that at any rate they are a *special* kind of word, which is distinguishable from other kinds. Their distinguishing feature is that they are used for evaluating something, that is for commending or condemning it.

It has to be admitted that even purely descriptive words *can* be used for commending. To cite a common non-moral example (H 1996e: 261): one might commend a certain hotel by saying that it faced the sea. But there is a difference between saying that the hotel faces the sea and saying that it is a good hotel, as we can easily see. Whether the fact that the hotel faces the sea commends it to someone depends on whether he likes hotels that face the sea. A person who did not like such hotels could without contradiction say that the hotel faced the sea but was not for that reason a good one. But he could not agree that it was a good hotel and still maintain that it was not a good one. To call it a good hotel *has* to be to commend it, whatever one's standards of goodness in hotels, unless one is using 'good' (as of course one can) in some 'inverted commas' or off-colour sense.

Once this is explained, I can see no difficulty in distinguishing evaluative words or uses of words from descriptive ones. A simple test is provided by Moore's well-known 'open question' argument (H 1996d). For any predicate P, if it is possible to ask 'Agreed, it is P, but is it wrong?' or 'It is P, but is it a good one?', and if a negative answer is not self-contradictory, then P is a purely descriptive predicate. If a definition of an evaluative word is to be naturalistic, then the *definiens* has to be purely descriptive in this sense.

4.5. There are various other objections that a naturalist might make to my argument, with which I must now deal. The first two of them concern a matter which I slid over too quickly earlier. I said, you remember, that the sort of actions that people applied words like 'wrong' to had to be specifiable in a morally neutral way. That was all right as far as it went. But I went further; I said that they had to be specifiable without appealing to anything but observable behaviour of the speaker and observable properties of the actions. But, it might be objected, a great many words are such that we cannot say what things people apply them to without appealing to more than observable behaviour and the observable properties of objects. It might be claimed that all words for so-called 'secondary qualities', such as colour words, fall into this class. For example, how do we tell what objects people apply the word 'red' to? Redness is on the face of it an observable property. But, it might be said, if we are to say correctly what people who know the language are applying it to, we have to say that they are applying it to things that *appear* in a certain way to them. For people are sometimes mistaken about what things are red. They may be white things in a red light, for example. Or the people may have suddenly gone colour-blind. In either of these cases, they are using the *word* correctly to describe *objects* which they mistakenly think are red. It is their observation that is at fault, not their use of the language.

If, accordingly, we are to distinguish genuine linguistic mistakes from faults in observation, we shall have, in the cases of the colour-blind and of those who are in a bad light, to distinguish incorrect *uses* of the word 'red' (that is, uses of it with a different meaning from that which it standardly has), from incorrect *applications* of it (that is, applications of it to objects to which it is not standardly applied). This is obviously no place to go into this very difficult question. We can avoid it by stipulating that in our linguistic research we take into account only *standard* uses of the words we are investigating: that is, only uses which are free from both linguistic and observational mistakes. And the only way, so far as I can see, to tell which uses are standard and free from both kinds of mistakes is to select a class of speakers who, we decide, make neither kind of mistake (at least on the occasions when we examine them) and to record *their* usage. We shall then no longer have, for our present purposes, to distinguish between use and application.

The effect of this stipulation will be that we shall get a class of speakers who all apply the word 'red' to the same objects, 'the same' being defined objectively in terms of standard conditions of use. And, we may rightly add in defence of the stipulation, there has to be this kind of standard use, if 'language is to be a means of communication' (Wittgenstein 1953: sec. 242; see H 1996*e*). This, we may admit at least for the sake of argument, *is* a condition for the successful use of words like 'red' in communication. We shall see later that this by no means applies to words like 'wrong', in spite of the efforts of descriptivists to persuade us that it does. But of words like 'red' it is *perhaps* true, though it has been argued (Lewis and Woodfield 1985) that the claim is not without its difficulties. So let us ask what would be the consequences for ethical theory if it *were* true of words like 'wrong'. There would then be a 'standard use' of these words, and all uses which deviated from this standard would be simply incorrect. So what I said about naturalism collapsing into relativism would be substantiated, and the objection we are considering would fail. For it is obvious that different cultures have different standard applications for the word 'wrong', as I showed earlier. And in each of the cultures conformity to their differing standard uses would be enough to secure correctness in moral judgement.

Let me cite an example which I have used before (H 1986*c*). Suppose that some deviant says that it is wrong not to love our enemies. If the people in his society have a standard application for the word 'wrong', according to which this (not loving our enemies) is not one of the things called wrong, they can simply write the deviant off as misusing the word 'wrong'. So the correctness of the application of moral words has to be assessed relative to the culture within which they are being used, and it becomes by definition impossible to preach moral reform. If we want to avoid this conclusion, we shall have to give up saying that moral properties are like secondary qualities such as 'red'.

4.6. So much for what I shall call the 'objection from secondary qualities'. Next, we have to consider the objection that I have been unfair in my choice of examples of applications of moral words. You will remember that I used examples like abortion and fighting. It might be objected that the moral statements that abortion, or that fighting, is wrong are not sufficiently basic, in a sense that I must explain. It might be alleged that if people call these kinds of acts wrong, they call them so, not because of what they are in themselves, but because they are infractions of some higher and more general principle which determines, in combination with certain factual premisses, that they are wrong. If this were so, then there would not, at the fundamental level, be the sort of moral disagreement on which I have been trading in my argument. The parties might disagree about the morality of fighting or of abortion, but only because they disagreed about the facts. They might agree, the objection goes on, on the wrongness of doing what results in the diminution of happiness or human flourishing, or in the failure to meet fundamental human needs; they differ only in that one side thinks that abortion (or fighting) would have this result, and the other thinks it would not.

Let us take first the 'fundamental human needs' formulation, which brings out well the difficulties of sustaining this kind of objection. I said earlier that, in order to be a true example of naturalism, an ethical theory had to specify in morally neutral terms the applications of a moral word which were to count as correct. We can now see how necessary this condition was. The question at issue is whether expressions like 'fundamental human needs' can ever be morally neutral. If they cannot, the naturalist will again turn into a relativist, as we shall see. But before that I have to make some remarks, not for the first time, about the word 'needs' (see H 1979h).

There is a dispute between those who think that needs can be absolute and those who think that all needs are relative to some end. That is, do all things needed have to be needed for some purpose, or can they be just needed? Certainly some are needed for a purpose. For example, I need transport to get to Stockholm; if I were not going anywhere, I would not need transport. Are there things needed which we do not need in order to do anything, or for any purpose? Etymology is on the side of those who deny this. The word 'need' in languages akin to German is closely linked with words for necessity. 'Need' in German is '*Not*', and this is cognate with '*notwendig*' and '*nötig*', both meaning 'necessary'. The same is true of Latin. This seems to indicate that for something to be a need is for it to be a necessary condition for obtaining something else.

On the other side, there are certainly instances in which we say that somebody needs something, but in which the question 'What for?' seems out of place. If somebody is 'in dire need' because of poverty, it is easy to think that he (or she) 'just needs' food, or help of some other kind. But this is a rather superficial argument. Obviously he needs food, say, in order to survive. So far the need is relative to an end. But, it will be said, *everybody* needs to survive; so there is an absolute need to survive lying behind the relative need for food. However, this is a mistake. Not everybody needs to survive. Some terminal patients in pain do not want to live, and would not say that they needed to live. Living is for them not a necessary condition for anything else that they want.

One might try to get over this difficulty by putting, in place of 'survival', some more general term like 'human flourishing'. This was first introduced, I think, as a translation of Aristotle's key term '*eudaimoniā*', commonly but incorrectly translated 'happiness'. I have already mentioned both terms. But Aristotle himself notes the indeterminacy of meaning of such phrases. He says:

since all knowledge and choice aims at some good, what is it at which we say politics aims, and what do we say is the highest of goods achieved by action? In name, at any rate, we might almost say that it is agreed by the great majority. For both the many and the better sort say it is *eudaimoniā*, and they understand 'living well' and 'doing well' as the same as this. But about what *eu-daimonia* is, they disagree, and the many do not give the same answer as the wise. (*Eth. Nic.* 1095ª14 ff.)

And Aristotle is obviously also aware that the term is not evaluatively neutral, as is shown by the equivalents he gives, 'living well' and 'doing well'. The latter is a notoriously ambiguous expression widely used by Plato (e.g. in the last two words, as well as in the second book, of the *Republic*). It can mean either 'acting well' or 'faring well'. Even the prefix of *eudaimonia* gives the game away; it is the same as is translated 'well' in the two other expressions. Perhaps the best literal translation of *eudaimonia* is 'having a good *daimōn*' (we might say, 'good fortune', a person's *daimōn* being his private deity, benign or malign as the case might be).

Those descriptivists who wish to insist on an absolute sense of 'need' cannot therefore appeal to Aristotle. For if people need food in order to flourish, there will be disputes about what counts as flourishing. And even if there were not, the move would not succeed. For although we might say that someone needs food, clothing, shelter, etc. in order to flourish, we cannot say that he *needs* to flourish. Everyone, perhaps, *wants* to flourish (though they may differ about what counts as flourishing). Indeed, it is perhaps an analytic truth that everybody wants to flourish, because 'I want not to flourish' sounds at least logically odd. But it is a misuse of language to say that someone *needs* to flourish. If we understand this at all, we shall be tempted to ask, in perplexity, 'What for?'; and it is not at all clear what the answer could be. This in itself is an indication that needs have to be relative to a purpose.

It follows from this that the naturalist move I have been discussing is bound to fail. For, as we saw, it is a condition for being a real naturalist that one gives the truth conditions of moral statements in terms of properties which are determinate, and can indeed be determined by observing the standard application of moral words. But suppose that the naturalist now claims that there *is* a standard application: 'morally wrong', for example, is applied to actions which deny to people their fundamental human needs. We have only to point out that there is no standard application for this latter expression—at least none that helps the descriptivist. Admittedly, 'needs' in its *relative* sense is standardly applied in cases where the question 'What for?' has an answer. But our naturalist is not appealing to those cases. He is appealing to alleged cases where the question is inappropriate. That is, the needs to which he is appealing have to remain needs *whatever* anybody's aims or purposes are. But if what I have just been saying is true, there are no such absolute needs. Even if everybody, analytically, wants to flourish, different people will count different kinds of life as flourishing; so the truth conditions of moral statements (the application rules for moral words) will vary from one person or at least from one culture to another, and the naturalist will again turn out to be a relativist.

4.7. I am conscious that many people will be dissatisfied with my argument so far. They will complain that although I have refuted particular kinds of naturalism, I have not precluded there being some kind which escapes these refutations. I did indeed set out a perfectly general argument to show that naturalism is bound to result in relativism. But the suspicion will remain that there might be some version of it which could avoid this consequence.

The only way I can think of to meet this objection is to choose, as a candidate for a viable naturalistic theory, a theory which seems to me most likely to avoid collapsing into relativism, and discuss it in more detail. The most plausible candidate for a definition of 'right action' is a utilitarian one. Such a definition has sometimes been attributed to J. S. Mill; but wrongly. The famous statement of his view at the beginning of his *Utilitarianism*, that actions are right in proportion as they tend to promote happiness, etc. (1861: ch. 2), is not intended as a definition but as a substantial claim about what actions *are* right. His view about the *meanings* of moral words is a clearly prescriptivist one, and is set out in Mill 1843, last chapter.

However, let us try out a utilitarian naturalistic definition, in a somewhat more up-to-date form. I will formulate it as follows: 'Right action' means 'action which maximizes the satisfaction, in sum, of the preferences of all affected parties.' This formulation has the advantage for my purposes that it seems to come as close as possible to the kind of non-naturalistic, non-descriptivistic utilitarianism which I myself favour; so the differences will be instructive. I could have said '. . . maximizes the furtherance, in sum, of the *interests* of all affected parties'; but I prefer the formulation in terms of preferences, because the word 'interests' is a very unclear one. It could be accused of being evaluative, and thus of spoiling the naturalistic credentials of the definition; but 'preferences' is all right, because it is clearly a matter of fact what people do prefer (although their preference is itself an evaluation on their part).

This kind of naturalism could be said to be subjectivistic, because preference is a subjective state. But I am not going to hold that against the definition; it is worth while examining it all the same. We must distinguish this definition from that which says that 'right action' means 'action which maximizes the satisfaction of *the speaker's* or *the agent's* preferences'. These definitions are versions of egoism, and I do not think that anybody would agree that that is what they *mean* by 'right action' if that is taken in its moral sense. The definition also runs up against Moore's argument already mentioned; it is clearly an open question whether an action which maximizes the satisfaction of the speaker's or the agent's preferences is the right action. But if we say 'all affected parties' the definition becomes a bit more plausible.

Such a definition is not so obviously relativistic as some we have discussed; for if we take into account *all* the preferences of *all* the affected parties, we shall get a unique answer to the question 'What is the right action?' whoever is answering it, and whatever his individual preferences are. I would therefore think this the most acceptable form of naturalism. It is somewhat similar to David Brink's (H 1996*e*). But there are still some things wrong with it, and I doubt whether in the end it escapes relativism. For if we imagine two people, one a utilitarian and one not, who for that reason say one of them that an action is right and the other that it is not, the same difficulties will arise as before. If the utilitarian says that his view is established by the very *meaning* of right, his opponent will reply that he himself does not mean the same by it; and then they will be left both saying what is true in *their own* different senses of 'right' (H 1996*d*). Such an impasse can only be avoided, I think, by reintroducing a *prescriptive* element into the meaning of 'right'; they will then be really contradicting one another, and can begin to discuss their dispute in a common language. How this is to be done, I shall leave until later (7.4 ff.).

There are also other difficulties with this utilitarian naturalistic definition. The first of these is that, although it sits easier with Moore's open question argument than the egoistic version, it is still not very happy. It does not seem self-contradictory to give a negative answer to the question 'The act would maximally satisfy the preferences of all affected parties, but is it right?' I have in my *MT* set out a two-level version of utilitarianism which does, I hope, enable us to avoid the counter-intuitive consequences that are claimed to afflict the utilitarian; but this simple naturalistic version seems to me to run headlong into them. On the face of it, there are plenty of actions which would maximize preference-satisfaction in sum, but which it would not be self-contradictory to call wrong.

My own theory does not say that 'right action' *means* 'action which maximally satisfies preferences'. Rather, it explains the meaning of such words as 'right' and 'wrong' and 'ought' as equivalent to various kinds of universalizable prescriptions or prohibitions, and only arrives at a utilitarian moral system by applying the logical properties of the words as so explained, *in combination with* certain other conceptual theses, to the world as we actually have it, and in particular to a world in which people have certain preferences. My version of utilitarianism has therefore both a formal and a substantial element. The formal element is provided, in part, by the universal-prescriptive definition of 'ought' and other moral words; but that is not the only element. There is also a substantial element which emerges in the application of this definition to the world. Prescriptivity plays an essential part in this construction of a utilitarian system. Since this prescriptivity is not available to a naturalist, he could not arrive at such a system. That is why my own system cannot rightly be accused of being naturalistic (*MT* 12.6).

But to explore further the question of how I myself avoid naturalism would be to digress from our present argument. I will content myself with saying that even the utilitarian form of naturalism, which I think is the most acceptable form, can hardly survive as an explanation of the *meaning* of moral words.

4.8. At this point I should perhaps say something about relativism itself, into which I have claimed that all the usual forms of naturalism collapse. Relativism is not in my narrow sense an ethical theory—that is, a theory about the meanings of moral words, or the nature of the moral concepts. I have said that certain ethical theories (naturalism in the present instance) collapse into relativism; but that is because they try to incorporate into their ethical theories theses of substance which do not belong there. The naturalist, for example, treats moral principles of substance as if they were no more than linguistic rules. As we saw, the moment we start treating them as moral principles of substance, which condemn one kind of behaviour and commend another, the naturalist gets caught in relativism, because he is saying that we have in a given culture to follow the rules of application of the moral words in use in that culture; and hence, if the rules are moral principles of substance (as they actually are, in spite of what the naturalist says), the members of each culture will be right in their moral opinions, however much these differ from culture to culture. But although ethical theories can stray into relativism by leaving the limits of ethical theory in the narrow sense, relativism itself, as I shall be using the term, is a substantial moral thesis: it says that whatever anybody says is wrong *is* wrong, and the same for 'right'. There are of course other senses of the word 'relativism', but this is the sense which I shall be using in what follows.

Although, however, relativism does not come into our taxonomy of ethical theories, it itself needs some taxonomy of its own, because it has to be divided into species. The main division is into what I shall call 'cultural relativism' and what I shall call 'individual relativism'. The first makes what is right and wrong relative to the opinions held in a given culture. The second makes it relative to the opinions of individuals, even within cultures. However, the main arguments against relativism apply to both species. There are, no doubt, many practical reasons why we should not embrace relativism; but I shall be concerned more with the theoretical troubles it gets into. In practice, if we were relativists, we should stop being able to say that people who thought that there was a duty to burn people whose religious views they disagreed with were wrong to think this; we could not say this even if the people they were burning were ourselves. I shall not say much about these obvious practical difficulties.

But this example brings out a theoretical difficulty as well. If I am tied to the stake and being burnt, I have, according to relativism, to say that the people who are burning me do right to do this, just because they think it right. But I shall also want, on my own part (together with my coreligionists), to say that they do wrong to burn me; and because I think this, I shall have to say, since I am a relativist, that I am right to think it. I shall therefore be saying that they are right to think it right, and also that I am right to think it wrong. But according to the logic of the words 'right' and 'wrong' as we actually use them, this is self-contradictory. For it is a logical property of the word 'right' as ordinarily used that I cannot without contradiction say that two people who say, one that an act is (all things considered) right, and the other that the same act is (all things considered) wrong, are both right.

As I said earlier, no harm might come of this kind of relativism at the theoretical level. The relativist would be left saying something which actually is self-contradictory if the words are used in their ordinary senses; but he might retort that he is not much concerned with our ordinary use of words, and he is recommending a new use according to which the statement in question is *not* self-contradictory. He might have difficulty in saying just what this new use was; but that would be his business.

But he is doing more than recommending a change in linguistic usage. He is implicitly still proposing to use the words 'right' and 'wrong' to commend and condemn actions. So he will be left having to agree both with someone (himself) who condemns the burning, and with someone else (the burners) who commend it. But if these are really substantial prescriptions for action (as in ordinary parlance they are), what shall we make of his statement? How shall we know what, if we agree with it, we are enjoined to do? We are apparently both enjoined to burn me and enjoined not to burn me. And what sort of prescription is that?

I have given an example in which it is two cultures that are in disagreement about the wrongness of an action. But the same difficulty would obviously arise in an even more acute form if it were two individuals who disagreed. If moral statements are prescriptive—that is, if the intention of those who make them is that we should act accordingly—then the adoption of relativism really would prevent moral language being a 'means of communication' between people in different cultures (as, indeed, MacIntyre has said it does, 1984; see H 1986c). In the assumption that we do need to have moral language for the particular kind of communication that we use it for (H 1987e), I conclude that relativism has to be rejected, and therefore that any ethical theory, like naturalism, which collapses into relativism has to be rejected too.

5

INTUITIONISM

5.1. In this chapter I have to deal with the second of the two possible types of descriptivism, which for want of a better name I am calling 'intuitionism'. You will remember that I distinguished this from naturalism, the other type of descriptivism. Naturalism, I said, is the view that the truth conditions of moral statements, which according to descriptivism determine their meaning, have to be the possession by actions, people, etc. of non-moral properties—that is, of properties specifiable in morally neutral terms. By contrast, intuitionism is the view that they are the possession of specifically moral, *sui generis* properties which cannot be defined without introducing some moral term into the *definiens*.

This means that the intuitionist is faced with a difficulty which the naturalist escapes. How is he to specify these properties, or these truth conditions, if he is forbidden to do so in non-moral terms? To revert to the project of linguistic research which I described in the last chapter: suppose that we are trying to determine what are the truth conditions, even within a single culture using a single language, of a moral statement. If we were trying to be naturalists, we could proceed as we do with ordinary non-moral words. We could, that is to say, look and see to what things people in the culture applied them, and then say that that was their correct application. This would involve being able to recognize the things the words were applied to as belonging to a determinate class. And the naturalist (at least the objectivist naturalist that we considered in Chapter 4) would have to claim that this could be done objectively. We could, I argued, do this with the word 'red' if there were a standard application of the word in the language. But if we are intuitionists, how are we to recognize the class of acts that a word like 'wrong' is applied to by speakers of the language? For on the face of it people speaking the same language apply the word 'wrong' to different and indeed inconsistent kinds of acts, as we saw. I cited as an example that some people call the act of fighting for one's country wrong, whereas others call this act right, and the act of not fighting when called on to do so wrong. This might be true even of a particular act of fighting in minutely specified circumstances on whose description the parties were agreed. The naturalist can make an attempt (unsuccessful, as we saw) to get out of this difficulty by suggesting that the word 'wrong' is being used by these people in different senses, because the applications are different. But what is the intuitionist to do?

It seems that, since he is not allowed to appeal to the observable non-moral properties of objects, there is nothing he can do except to say that the researcher just can recognize the class of actions that people call wrong. How is he to recognize them? Only, it would seem, by having the ability or capacity to recognize them. Modern intuitionists often deny that they are committed to any special 'faculty of intuition'; they deny that they are moral sense theorists—and we can well understand why they deny this; for such a moral sense is obviously suspect. And it may be true, since the word 'intuitionist' is used in so many different senses these days, that some intuitionists, in some senses of the word, can avoid positing such a faculty. But if so, they will have to explain how a linguistic researcher could determine the truth conditions of moral statements. At any rate, it should be clear by now that an intuitionist, in the sense in which I am using the term (that is, a descriptivist who says that, syntax apart, the meaning of moral statements is wholly determined by their truth conditions, and that the truth conditions cannot be specified in terms of non-moral properties)—that an intuitionist, so defined, cannot do without such a faculty. For unless a linguistic researcher possessed such a faculty, the class of actions that people called wrong would be quite indeterminate, and so his research would be quite inconclusive: the truth conditions of moral statements might be almost anything.

5.2 I now want to consider the view—which is at first sight plausible—that there is indeed such a faculty—that is, that we can, most of us, recognize actions that are wrong and actions that are not. Let us take a very obvious example. I have just filled up at a self-service petrol (gas) station that has no automatic machine to exact the cash before one fills up, and am wondering whether to go and pay the cashier for my petrol, or just to drive away without paying. The cashier is not looking, nor is anybody else. If I am like most people, when I contemplate doing this, I get a quite easily recognizable experience. Let us call it the thought (even the conviction) that it would be wrong to do it. So here, at any rate, we seem to have a clear case of recognizing a (proposed) act as wrong. So an intuitionist might claim that there *is* this faculty by which we can recognize wrong acts.

With this, taken in one sense, few will disagree. Moral philosophers of all persuasions—be they descriptivists or non-descriptivists, objectivists or subjectivists, even emotivists—will at once recognize something that is going on in the mind of the person in this predicament. I certainly recognize it myself. They will call it by different names. An intuitionist will call it the thought or conviction that the act would be wrong. A subjectivist naturalist is likely to call it a *feeling* of disapproval of the proposed act. An emotivist will probably use the same expression; and I myself see no harm in using it. So it looks as if they all agree that this experience occurs, and disagree only in what they call it. Is there then only a verbal difference between what the intuitionists say about the experience, and what the others say?

If there is no *experiential* difference between the feeling or thought that the person has according to the intuitionists, and that which he has according to, say, an emotivist, what other difference could there be? We might suggest that there is a logical difference—that is, a difference in the logical properties attributed by these different thinkers to the statement that this feeling or thought (whichever it is) occurs, and to the moral statement which is made on the ground that it occurs (namely the statement that the act would be wrong). To this suggestion we shall recur later in this chapter. But for the moment I want to point out that there are other moral situations which are much more difficult for the intuitionist. In the petrol station case, we all, or nearly all, agree that the act would be wrong. There may be some reprobates who do not agree that it would be wrong; but they are probably few enough for us to ignore them, just as, in studying the standard use of an ordinary descriptive word like 'red', we ignore those few who use it incorrectly. But all cases are not like the petrol station case.

The intuitionist is on the firmest ground in cases where we nearly all agree. But in many cases (those which give us trouble, and which moral philosophers ought to be helping us with) there *is* no such general agreement. When we are thinking about fighting for one's country, or about abortion, or about eating meat, some of us have the recognizable thought or feeling and some do not. It would not be much of a victory for the intuitionist to show that, in cases where we all think we know the answers to moral questions, we all have the same thought or feeling, if in many other cases—and those which cause us most trouble in our moral thinking—we have different thoughts or feelings. For it is the latter class of cases in which we really need to be told the truth conditions of moral statements, so that we can find out which of them are true.

Reverting, then, to our linguistic researcher: it looks as if there is nothing he can do, if he wishes to learn to recognize the class of actions that are being called wrong, except to employ *his own* faculty of moral intuition. In a way this makes his task easier. Instead of, as a conscientious naturalist would have to, laboriously cataloguing, in non-moral terms, the classes of actions that *other people* call wrong, he can perhaps forget about other people, and just look at the actions that he himself calls wrong. For the object of his research is to give the truth conditions of moral statements. Since he has this faculty, he knows already what the truth conditions are. The truth condition of a statement that an act is wrong is that it should produce in him this recognizable reaction. Can he then stop studying what other people say?

5.3. The intuitionist might reply that this is going too fast. Suppose, he might say, that I discover that most other people apply the word 'wrong' to some kind of act to which I do not apply it. Shall I not then begin to think that my faculty of moral intuition is faulty? Shall I not even begin to *change* my perception of what is right and wrong, so as to conform with the others, at least if they are people whom in general I respect? So, although I go on saying that the truth conditions of moral statements are that acts, etc. should be perceived

by *me* as right or wrong, *what* is perceived by me as right or wrong
will change, to become more like what *other people* call right or wrong.
This process is even clearer in the moral education of children, who,
let us suppose, start off without *any* moral opinions or perceptions,
and who therefore have to get all their moral opinions initially from
other people, their elders or later their contemporaries, whom they
respect. This is indeed, we may agree, how the mores of a given culture become to some degree homogeneous.

Some intuitionists might dissent from this, and claim that there
are moral opinions which are innate, or which at least develop independently of the moral opinions of other people. If so, it is pretty obvious that different moral opinions are innate in the members of
different cultures, at least on matters which are disputed between
those cultures. This would be hard to explain genetically. However,
we might agree at least that there is an innate disposition to think
morally—a disposition which does not determine the *content* of a person's morality, but at least partly determines its *form*. This would tally
with Chomsky's view that there are 'universals' (as they are called) of
language which are genetically determined and common to all cultures (1965: 35). According to this suggestion, there is a common
structure of moral language, with its grammar and its logic, which
we are all genetically disposed to learn, and therefore learn more
easily than if we had no such genetic predisposition. Such a view is
consistent with my own, but I express no opinion on whether it is
right; that would have to be determined by empirical research. The
important thing is that even if the *form* of morality is innate, that is
consistent with morality having very different *contents* in different
cultures, just as the view that grammar and even logic is innate is
consistent with the members of those cultures having very different
factual opinions about what goes on in earth or heaven.

For this reason an intuitionist could not draw much comfort from
the existence, if it did exist, of a common or (in the linguists' sense)
universal moral language with its logic. For he wants to claim not
only that the form of morality is common between cultures, but that
its content is. This is in any case a highly implausible claim. Perhaps
the intuitionist would be willing to draw in his horns a bit, and claim

only that there are important *elements* that are common to the moralities of different cultures. That may well be true: most cultures condemn murder, for example (though what they count as murder varies). However, the intuitionist explanation of these common elements is not the only possible one. It may be the case (I think it is) that the existence of a common moral 'grammar' or 'logic' has led to moral thinkers in all cultures coming to the same conclusions. This would be consistent with my own account of moral thinking which I shall be summarizing later. It by no means establishes that there are common moral perceptions which all cultures share. The common elements might be arrived at by reason and not by intuition.

5.4. I return then to our programme of linguistic research into the truth conditions of moral statements, or the application conditions of moral predicates. The intuitionist view, stated baldly, is that wrongness, for example, is a common property shared by many actions, which is discernible by those who have the necessary power of discernment. We considered the objection that if this were so, I could simply ignore the opinions of other people, and rely on my own power of discernment. This objection we answered on behalf of the intuitionist by suggesting that even if we thought we had this power, we might come to doubt its reliability if our moral opinions conflicted with those of other people. This might, we suggested, lead us to *change* our perceptions of right and wrong to conform to those of other people that we respected.

But now look where this is leading the intuitionist, if he takes this line. It turns out that we have to rely, not on our own power of discernment, but on a consensus between the deliverances of the intuitions of people whom we respect. We shall presumably respect those people whose moral opinions *in general* we share. We shall be willing to adapt *particular* opinions to conform to the others; but if anyone had moral opinions differing radically and over a wide area of morality from our own, we should be unlikely to respect him (or her). The intuitionist seems likely to have to say that our source for the truth conditions of moral statements is not our own individual faculty of recognition of moral properties, but rather a consensus of like-minded people in recognizing them.

That intuitionists might be led to take this line is suggested by what has frequently happened in arguments between them and their opponents. There is a well-worn argument against intuitionism called 'the argument from moral disagreement'. The argument goes like this. There undoubtedly are cases in which people's moral opinions disagree. Therefore the two parties cannot both be right. So, if moral intuitions are a reliable source of moral truth, one or other party must lack this source. That party, therefore, has an intuition which is faulty (or, if you refuse to call it an intuition if it is faulty, does not have the power of intuition—it does not matter for the argument which way we put it). But the intuitionist has given us no way of determining *which* of the two parties has a faulty intuition. It would be obviously and viciously circular to try to settle the matter by having a further intuition that one of the parties has a reliable intuition and the other not; for this further intuition could in turn be challenged by the party who had been put down by it. And it would be no better to call in the intuitions of third or fourth parties, for they too could be challenged in the same way. So, the objection goes on, intuitionism will yield no determinate answer to disputed moral questions.

It has been common for intuitionists to say, in reply to this objection, that not all intuitions (or supposed intuitions) are reliable, but only those of 'thoughtful and well-educated people' (W. D. Ross 1930: 41). We should follow *their* intuitions in preference to those of people who have not been well educated. But recall what I said earlier about the relation between intuitions and moral education. It is perfectly true that people's intuitions (that is their moral convictions) will vary according to how they have been educated. But what are we claiming when we claim that only the intuitions of well-educated people are reliable? I said that we are likely to make our own moral opinions or perceptions conform to those of people whom we respect, and that this was especially evident in the moral education of children, who start, we supposed, with no determinate moral opinions. If this is true, and if the intuitionist says we should respect only the moral intuitions of well-educated people, another obvious circularity appears in his argument. For who is to count as well educated? Suppose that, as may well happen in a dispute about, say, meat-eating, both parties indignantly maintain that they have been well educated. How can we adjudicate between them? Obviously not by calling in further intuitions about what is a good education.

You will now see, I hope, why I said in Chapter 4 that intuitionism, like naturalism, collapses inevitably into relativism. The point is that the general consensus on moral questions which is likely to exist in a given culture is the result of a common moral education. In closed and morally homogeneous cultures this consensus is likely to cover all or nearly all moral questions. But even in a pluralist society like our own it is likely to cover a great many questions, some of them fundamental. However, if *any* of these common moral opinions is challenged by a moral reformer, it is no use appealing to the consensus itself to validate the opinions. If I may quote a telling passage from Dryden:

> By education most have been misled;
> So they believe, because they were so bred.
> The priest continues what the nurse began:
> And thus the child imposes on the man. (1637, pt. 3, 389)

Intuitions are relative to cultures. As I have said, I do not deny for a moment that intuitions will be found which are common to most or even to nearly all cultures, like that forbidding murder (though, as I also said, murder is not defined in the same way in all cultures). But even if this is so, if anybody *were* to challenge this consensus, we could not rule him out of court by appealing to the consensus. True, most people have the intuitions, and we say that those who do not have them were not well brought up. But we say this only because we ourselves have been brought up in the way that we have been. If we had been brought up in a different way, we might have agreed with the dissident. Perhaps, if he is successful in his moral reform, future generations may be brought up in his way rather than in ours. This is unlikely to happen with murder, because there are good *reasons* (not based on intuition) for condemning murder. How we should reason about such questions, I shall be explaining later. But the good reasons do *not* consist in the fact that there is a consensus. And when we come to fighting or to meat-eating or to abortion, there *is* no consensus to appeal to, and we have to find a way of reaching one by argument, not by intuition. Intuition by itself is no prophylactic against relativism.

5.5. I am now going on, as I promised, to discuss the variety of naturalism called subjectivism. We have now reached a point at which it can easily be made clear how very close intuitionism is to subjectivism. Indeed, we can see that when its pretended objectivist trappings have been stripped off, intuitionism *is* a kind of subjectivism. It is not surprising, therefore, that intuitionism collapses into relativism. I said in the preceding chapter that relativism is not an ethical theory in my narrow sense, because it is about matters of moral substance (about what we ought to do) and not about what moral words mean. Subjectivism *is* a theory about what moral words mean. Its relation to relativism is that it makes relativism analytically true. Subjectivism is the view that when I am making a moral statement, I am saying simply that, as a matter of psychological fact, I (the speaker) approve or disapprove of some act or person. There is an alternative version according to which what I am saying is that *people in my society* approve or disapprove. This version I shall leave aside for the present, although similar objections can be made to it.

Subjectivism is a form of naturalism, because it gives the truth conditions of moral statements without introducing any moral terms into the *definiens*. The statement that as a matter of psychological fact I approve of an act contains no moral terms. It is an empirical statement verifiable either by introspection or by observation of my behaviour. It is important not to be confused here. To approve of something may be to have a moral opinion. But the *statement that* I approve is not itself a moral statement, even if made by myself. Someone, or even I myself, could *describe* my moral opinions, feelings, attitudes, etc. without saying anything moral. It is confusion on this point that has made many people mix up certain forms of non-descriptivism with subjectivism, as we shall see. Subjectivism, in the sense I am using, is one kind of naturalistic descriptivism; it can therefore not be any kind of non-descriptivism. It falls on the opposite side from non-descriptivism of the main divide between ethical theories that I set out in Chapter 3. Both when I was discussing objectivistic naturalism and when I was discussing intuitionism the fact of moral disagreement played a crucial role in my argument. This will be the case with subjectivism too. The recurrence of this fact of moral disagreement in arguments against all these theories is no accident. Because they are all in essence relativistic theories, it is inevitable that the fact of moral disagreement should play a part in arguments to show this. I shall be discussing shortly the relation between the roles of moral disagreement in arguments against these different theories. But its role in arguments against subjectivism, at least, is familiar. It is this. If I say that some act is wrong and you say that it is not wrong, then, according to subjectivism, I am making a statement of psychological fact about my own mental state or attitude, and you are making a statement of psychological fact about yours. But these statements are quite consistent with each other; whereas the original statements that the act is wrong, and that the act is not wrong, are not consistent with each other. The subjectivist must therefore be mistaken about what the statements mean.

This argument is so familiar, going back to Moore (1912: ch. 3) and indeed to Sidgwick and to some older moralists, that I do not need to dwell on it. It was Stevenson's attempt to avoid this objection to subjectivism that led him to his variety of non-descriptivism—he said that there was a disagreement in attitude though not in belief (1942, 1945: 3). It is a rather elementary mistake to think that the same argument can be turned against non-descriptivism. This is part of the general confusion, still too common, between subjectivism and non-descriptivism; but that will have to be left until later.

5.6. For the present I want just to draw your attention to the different ways in which the fact of moral disagreement figures in the arguments against objectivistic naturalism, subjectivistic naturalism, and intuitionism respectively. In the case of objectivistic naturalism the crucial point was that, since people disagree in their moral opinions, any attempt to establish a *single* set of truth conditions for moral statements by looking at what actions, etc. they apply moral predicates to will founder on this disagreement. We simply shall not get a consistent set of truth conditions. At best, we shall be left giving *different* sets of truth conditions for different cultures. If the naturalist tries to escape this objection by saying that the words mean different things when used in different cultures (or even by different individuals within a single culture), then he will be open to a very similar objection to that which we have just been making against the subjectivist; he will be admitting that the words do not mean the same in the mouths of these opposing parties, and that therefore their moral statements do not contradict one another, which obviously they do.

In the case of intuitionism, the trouble is basically the same. If we think that we can establish the truth conditions of moral statements by appeal to a faculty of moral intuition—by saying, that is, that those moral statements are true which are certified as true by this faculty—then we shall again get different answers, according to whose intuitions we examine. True, there is a difference between the cases of objectivist naturalism and intuitionism. In the case of intuitionism, there are not different sets of truth conditions. There is only one set, that is, conformity with intuition. But since the intuitions themselves conflict, we shall still get variation in the truth values of particular moral statements, depending on who is doing the judging. So the end result is the same, namely relativism. Subjectivism has the virtue of displaying this fault, which all these theories commit, in stark clarity. According to it, the person who makes a moral statement is simply reporting on his own psychological state. This, like intuitionism, yields a single set of truth conditions: if the psychological state is that which in fact the speaker has, then the statement is true. But—and this too is like intuitionism—we shall get no consistent answer about the truth of particular moral statements, because the answers will depend on whom we ask and what attitude he has.

5.7. I said that it was no accident that all these theories are in the same trouble, or at least in closely related troubles. I want now to bring this out even more clearly if I can, by examining the cases of intuitionism and subjectivism, and showing how similar they really are. This will be repugnant to intuitionists, who often think of themselves as objectivists, indeed as model or paradigm objectivists. But we can bring out the similarity by asking what intuitionists think the difference is between having an intuition and having a feeling or attitude of approval or disapproval. I gave an example earlier of a person who was thinking of driving away from a petrol station without paying. What, I asked, is the difference, other than a merely verbal one, between what intuitionists say about this situation and what subjectivists say? Certainly the *experience* that they are both attributing to the person is the same. It is the having of an attitude of disapproval, or the having of a conviction that the act would be wrong; but what is the difference? I can see no objection to saying that those who have moral convictions have moral attitudes, and vice versa. It ought to be agreed on all sides that the person in my example has both these things, or rather that they are the same thing.

The intuitionists are relying, in order to give us knowledge of moral truths, on a certain experience, which they call the having of a moral intuition. But the trouble is that such experiences are something *subjective*. If I have this experience, then I have it; there is absolutely nothing that can be appealed to, outside the experience itself, which could show whether it was really so or not. If I have this experience, I cannot be mistaken in thinking that I have it. This, indeed, is the attraction, in one way, of the intuitionist theory, just as it was the attraction of the sense-datum theories that used to be so popular in epistemology. Here is something that cannot be disputed: I have the experience called 'an intuition that a certain act would be wrong', and that is all there is to be said. Whatever may happen to anybody else, I have this experience, and, on the strength of it, according to the intuitionists, I am entitled to say that the act would be wrong.

But for this indisputability of the intuition we pay too heavy a price. For if nothing outside the experience can count against the existence of the intuition—if, that is to say, the mere having of the experience is the guarantee that it exists—then, by the same token, it cannot tell us about anything outside the actual experience. *All* that we can be certain of, by having this experience, is that we have it.

What this comes to is that, for all the sound and fury that went on in the battle between the people who called themselves 'objectivists' (that is, the intuitionists) and those whom they called 'subjectivists', there was nothing of substance that really divided them. The intuitionists *thought* that, according to their theory, to say that an act is wrong was not just to report on a subjective fact. But they were not justified in saying this. For according to their theory the mere occurrence of the experience which they called an intuition (and which the subjectivists called a feeling or attitude of disapproval) is the guarantee that a certain moral statement is true. That is *the* truth condition of the moral statement. But if so, then the moral statement cannot say any more than that the experience occurs. If the mere occurrence of the experience guarantees the truth of the moral statement, then there cannot be any more to making the statement than there is to saying that the experience occurs.

The intuitionists did not see this, because they wanted to maintain, at the same time as the position I have just been discussing (namely that the mere occurrence of the experience guarantees the truth of the moral statement), another position which is really incompatible with it. They wanted to maintain, as well, that the moral statement was 'objective'. What this meant, I am not sure; but in this context to call a moral statement objective entails at least the following: that if two people make, one of them a certain moral statement, and the other its negation (for example, that an act is wrong, and that it is not wrong), then they cannot both be right. It is impossible consistently to agree with both their statements. I hope you will note that in *this* sense I am myself an objectivist.

Intuitionists, in fact, very frequently insisted on this, that both cannot be right. But now you can see that this is inconsistent with the other thesis they maintained, namely that the mere occurrence of the experience guarantees the truth of the moral statement. For if this latter thesis is true, then, as we have seen, the person who has the experience, and says, accordingly, that an act is wrong, is really saying no more than that he has the experience; and he cannot be mistaken about *that*. If he were saying more, then the mere occurrence of the experience could not guarantee the truth of this more. However, on the 'objectivist' thesis just mentioned, the speaker must be saying more. For he is saying at least that, if anybody else thinks that the act is not wrong, he is mistaken to think this. If the objectivist thesis is true, this must be so; if, of two people who maintain, one of them that an act is wrong, and the other that it is not wrong, both cannot be right, then, in saying that an act is wrong, I must be implying that anybody who says otherwise is not right, that is, is mistaken.

We can see, therefore, that the alleged self-guaranteeingness of intuition is really incompatible with its alleged objectivity. But the self-guaranteeingness is what is really characteristic of intuition. There are other kinds of objectivism. I have already talked about object-ivistic naturalism, and when I come on in later chapters to non-descriptivism, I shall show that one can have an objectivist but non-descriptivist theory (my own) which maintains, at least, that of two people who disagree about a moral statement both cannot be right, or that it is impossible consistently to agree with both. Since there are non-intuitionist but still objectivist theories, it must be the self-guaranteeingness of moral intuitions that intuitionists have to hang on to, if they are going to retain what is essential in intuitionism. But since this is incompatible with their objectivism, they have, in order to be consistent, to give up the objectivism. And this means, as I said, that the only way in which intuitionists can remain intuitionists and avoid self-contradiction is to embrace some form of subjectivism.

5.8. This is perhaps an appropriate place to mention very briefly a topic which I have dealt with at length elsewhere (H 1955*a*, 1994*b*, *FR* 2.2 ff.) and which needs to be cleared up if we are to have an adequate taxonomy of ethical theories. It concerns a division between ethical theories which cuts across the classification we have been outlining. This means that, although it does affect intuitionism, it also affects a number of other ethical theories, both descriptivist and non-descriptivist. This is the division between what I shall call *particularist* and what I shall call *universalist* theories. It is very easily illustrated by talking of intuitionists in particular. About *what* do they think that moral statements have, in the first instance, to be made? That is, what are the objects of moral intuitions? We find among intuitionist writers some who stress the need to assess particular, that is individual, actions morally, but others who think that moral statements have to be made, not about individual actions, but about *kinds* of action. This ought to make a big difference to how we approach moral thinking.

One approach is to look at individual datable actions by individual identifiable people, and to ask whether they are right or wrong. Then we can arrive at more general moral principles by an inductive process. If lying has been perceived to be wrong in a lot of instances, for example, we may then generalize and form the hypothesis that all actions of that kind, namely lies, are wrong. The other approach is to start by considering *types* of actions, and decide whether actions of that type are wrong, thus forming for ourselves general moral principles; after that we can determine whether particular actions are wrong by asking whether they fall under those principles. For example, we first determine that lying is wrong, and then infer that to say a particular thing would be wrong, because it would be a lie.

But this statement of the difference is oversimplified. I used the word 'general', which has led a lot of moral philosophers into confusion, through being used as if it were synonymous with 'universal', though in fact there are two quite different concepts to be distinguished (see 7.7, H 1972*a*, 1994*b*, MT 2.5). Generality is the opposite of specificity and is a matter of degree. Universality contrasts, rather, with particularity, and is not a matter of degree. The two prescriptions 'One ought never to tell lies' and 'One ought never to tell lies to business partners' are both equally universal, in that *any* act which falls under the description 'lies' or 'lies told to business partners' (and note that these descriptions are in universal terms) is prohibited by the respective prescriptions. But the first is much more general, much less specific, than the second.

A particularist has to decide whether he is objecting to our making moral statements about *general* types of cases, and asking us to make them only, in the first instance, about very *specific* cases; or whether he is insisting that no *universal* terms, even highly specific ones, are to be used in the descriptions of the cases we are making our moral statements about. That is, is he insisting that all moral statements have to be, in the first instance, about individual acts identified in some other way than by describing them in universal terms, however specific; or is he allowing us to make them about kinds of cases described in universal terms, provided that the terms are highly specific?

I am a universalist, though not an intuitionist universalist. That is,

I think that moral statements are always made about actions, etc. because of universal properties that they have. This by no means entails that those properties have to be describable in very general terms (that is, in unspecific, simple terms which do not go into great detail). So, if I *were* an intuitionist, I would support the universalist version of the theory. Once universality is distinguished from generality, most of the plausibility of particularism disappears. What particularists are after is usually specificity: they do not want us to make our moral statements on the basis of very general descriptions of actions, such as 'lying', but want to be allowed to take account, in their moral thinking, of the details of cases, which may, they think, be highly relevant. With this I agree; it is often necessary to discuss cases in considerable detail before we pronounce on them. But this does not stop my saying that it is still the universal, though highly specific, properties of the cases that are the grounds of our moral statements, and not the mere fact that those individuals are involved in them.

I do not need here to enlarge on the division of ethical theories into particularist and universalist theories. But I had to make this distinction in order to make my taxonomy complete. It is perhaps worth mentioning, as I have elsewhere (H 1955a, 1994b), that the possibility of making moral statements about fictional characters is a strong argument against particularism; for fictional characters can only be described in universal terms; they do not exist to be pointed to as individuals.

A short way with particularism is to say that there cannot be anything about an action which makes it wrong, or about a person which makes him bad, except such features as are specifiable in universal terms. Any feature which was not so specifiable would have to be some individual essence or haecceity which was not describable except by saying 'this person' or 'this act', and remaining silent thereafter. But this is not to describe an act or a person at all. The only way to describe a person or act is to attribute universal properties to him or it. And these have to include the reasons for calling the person bad or the act wrong. The particularist cannot reply by substituting, for 'this person' or 'this act', 'exactly like this person' or 'exactly like this act', because this would turn the description into one in terms of universal properties after all (H 1955a, *FR* 2.2). But this is not the place to enter into such metaphysical tangles.

However, this way is too short a way. It is too short, because there are universal properties which are relational, connoting relations to an individual, such as 'mother of', and 'lover of'. In the expression 'mother of James', 'James' denotes an individual. But all the same the duties one may have to one's mother may be universal properties shared with anybody who is a child, or a child of a specific kind.

That is why prudential self-interested judgements are universalizable after a fashion. They are judgements about relations to an individual, namely oneself. If I ought, prudentially speaking, to do a certain thing in a certain precise situation, then anybody who is in the same situation would be well advised, in prudence, to do the same thing. For example, if it would be in my interest to tell the truth (make a clean breast of it), the situation being what it is, then it would be in the interest of any similar person in a similar situation to do the same, that is, speak the truth. The same holds if for 'speak the truth' we substitute 'tell a lie', though in that case the moral and the prudential judgements may diverge. If it is in the interest of one person to tell a lie, it would be in the interest of any precisely similar person in precisely the same situation to tell a lie.

However, we are concerned now, not with prudence (i.e. what I ought to do in my own interest), but with what I ought to do because of my relations with *other* individuals, for example, duties to my mother because she is my mother. J. E. Hare (1996: 151 f.) has rightly distinguished between different types of universalizability. There is universalizability over all agents, but there is also universalizability over all recipients (e.g. victims); and there are other senses too in which judgements may be universalizable. A judgement may be universalizable in one of these senses but not others. For example, a prudential judgement is universalizable over agents, but not over recipients. It relates to *my* interest as agent, but not to my interest as recipient: I can treat other recipients just as I please, provided that *my own* interest is secured by my action.

The fact that relations to individuals may be universal *qua* relations (they are two-or-more-place universal predicates, although the individuals themselves are not universal) opens the door to a great many duties about which we may be in doubt whether to call them *moral* duties at all. For example, are my duties to my country, because it is *my* country, moral duties, or only, to use an expression of Simon Blackburn's (1984: 186), *shmoral* duties? In other words, are they duties which can be fully universalized over all *recipients* in all situations, or only over all *agents*. And if I have moral duties to *my* country, have I moral duties to *my* family, or *my* tribe, or *my* sex, or *my* species (for short, to my own set) which are not owed to other people's sets? I can certainly have a moral duty to keep *my* promises, and not other people's promises (H 1992*e*: ii. 1259). This would obviously endanger one of the main props of the type of moral argument that I advocate.

The Kantian solution to this problem is presumably (if I may put words into Kant's mouth) that I have only such duties to *my* family as I am willing to allow other similar people to have to *their* families. And the same is true if for 'family' we substitute any of the other restricted sets I have mentioned. Blackburn has suggested to me in conversation that the difference between himself and me can be put in terms of the difference between Hume and Kant. I think I am still a follower of Kant, and Blackburn of Hume. The advantage that Kant has over Hume is that Hume cannot make the move I have just made. He relies on *human* sympathy as the foundation of morality, whereas Kant relies on the wills of all rational beings.

In this connection it may be useful to recall points made by Peter Singer and by Derek Parfit. Singer has suggested (1981: ch. 4) that the ability to reason, itself genetically useful and therefore fostered by evolution, can, as it were, take hold and push us beyond what the interest of our genes requires. Thus we can find no good reason for stopping at the interests of our own village or tribe. It is in our own interest and that of our genes to preserve members of our own tribe; but it is hard to stop there. And so reason encourages us to go further, and seek to promote the interests of other tribes and even other species. I have myself suggested that what is true of the faculty of reason may be true of the gift of language which is its vehicle (H 1981*b*). So perhaps moral language is after all superior to shmoral language.

Parfit too (1984: chs. 6 ff.) argues for an extension of our concern beyond narrow self-interest. He says that the same arguments by which prudence prevails over the 'present aim theory' can be used to give the victory to universal morality over prudence. If we may extend what he says a little, they may also be used to give the victory to Kant over Hume. That is to say, although singular terms are admissible in moral judgements, they have to be governed by a universal rule which allows *anybody* so related to an individual or set to have similar duties to that individual or set.

If Parfit and Singer are right, then we have a solution to the problem of shmoralities. They can count as moralities only if they are governed by such a universal rule. But shmoralities are not ruled out by logic, any more than prudence is. I admitted in *MT* 11.2 ff. that consistent amoralism is a viable option, and the same is true of shmoralism. And in *MT* 1.5 I admitted that alternative languages are available for those who are unwilling to use the moral language. The extreme case is the plain imperative, the language expressing simple individual desires or 'present aims'. But there are other kinds of shmoral language in between this and the language of morals. The question is, 'Why should we use the moral language in preference to these?' I am sure that I myself prefer to use moral language, and can therefore follow Moore (1903: 6) and say that in the sense that I use it, the moral judgements in it are universalizable.

I am equally sure that Blackburn and I shall find ourselves in agreement in most of our moral judgements, though it is not clear to me how he would argue for them. He would probably invoke Hume, whose views do not diverge from Kant's as much as is commonly supposed, either in epistemology or in ethics, although their characters were very different. We shall see in 7.3 that arguability, and with it the possibility of reconciling conflicting moral positions, are a requirement for a satisfactory ethical theory. This is what renders objective moral prescriptions, acceptable to all rational thinkers, possible (H 1993*g*). Shmoral prescriptions, by contrast, though they may be rationally acceptable to agents, as conducive to their interests and those of their own sets, may be expected not to be acceptable to their victims, who cannot, as Kant put it, share the ends of the prescribed actions (8.2).

This is one reason why I prefer to use the moral language. Another reason is prudential in the broadest sense. I said in *MT* 11.2 ff. that if we were bringing up a child with no thought of anything but the child's own interest, we should bring him up to use moral language and follow moral prescriptions. Having seen the terrible things that have been done throughout the ages, and right up to the present day, in the cause of shmoral systems that are not moral in the full sense, I feel an urge to solve our problems by appeal to morality. That perhaps is the only way, especially for dealing with problems of our relations to other species.

For clarity we must distinguish between two questions: the question of what the logic of the moral, as opposed to the shmoral, language requires, and the question of how to motivate people to use it. If I am right in my answer to the first question, the second still remains. But this is not a question for ethical theory in the narrow sense. I cannot so far see the solution to these problems, and have therefore to leave some unfinished business, as I did in *FR* 7.4 and *MT* 5.6. I have since then tied up some loose ends, and I hope that I or others will tie up more. That is one reason why I have left a corner of my taxonomy open for those that come after (6.7). But at present I feel inclined to support Kant against Hume.

5.9. We are now at the end of my discussion and classification of descriptivist theories. We found that they all have something wrong with them: the common fault that they share is that they all inevitably, if fully examined, collapse into relativism. This, as I say, is a surprising result, because the main motive of most descriptivists has been the desire to *avoid* relativism. But they have gone the wrong way about avoiding it. It is in fact only by abandoning descriptivism that we can attain a kind of objectivity in our moral statements, as we shall see. I think that Kant understood this. It is because when we are thinking morally we are looking for *prescriptions* for action, not *descriptions* of actions, that our thinking is constrained (H 1996c). There are certain *maxims* (to use Kant's word) which we cannot *will* to become universal laws; and maxims are a kind of prescriptions.

To anticipate what I shall be saying later: the reason why a prescriptivist theory can avoid collapsing into relativism is that the prescriptive element in the meaning of moral statements, and especially its *form*, can be shared between cultures with different mores, as the descriptive meaning cannot. It is because all the different cultures are prescribing, and prescribing in a universal form (they *share* that part of the meaning of their moral statements) that they are all constrained in their reasoning by the formal logical properties of what they are saying, which are the same whatever the content of their moral opinions. But you may not understand this until I come to outline my own theory.

In the next chapter I shall be going over to the other side of the main division of ethical theories, and classifying non-descriptivist theories. I shall start with emotivism, of which Axel Hägerström was a pioneer, and discuss its merits and faults, the main fault being that it leads to irrationalism and makes any at all fundamental moral reasoning impossible. Then I shall present a theory which avoids this fault, and also the faults of descriptivism.

6

EMOTIVISM

6.1. In Chapter 5 I finished, for the time being, talking about descriptivist theories. We saw that they were all destined to collapse into relativism, which is the reverse of what most of their supporters wish. I am going in Chapters 6 and 7 to talk about non-descriptivist theories, and ask whether they can avoid this collapse into relativism. Surprisingly (to some people), we shall discover that it is a non-descriptive element in the meaning of moral statements which can enable a non-descriptivist theory to avoid relativism (7.3). But this element was not well characterized by the first of the non-descriptivist kinds of theory I shall discuss, namely emotivism. However, the proponents of emotivism, of whom Axel Hägerström (1911) was the first in modern times, made the important step of suggesting that there *is* another element in the meaning of moral statements besides their syntax and their truth conditions. If they had not made this step, the later advances towards an objectivist ethical theory would have been impossible; for descriptivism has to be rejected before this step can be made.

I shall in what follows be criticizing emotivism in general, and not any particular emotivist, and certainly not Hägerström. Since many of the modern emotivists make errors which are not essential to emotivism itself, it will be best if I construct my own version of an emotivist theory which brings out most clearly the virtues and the faults in emotivism. I do not intend this as a caricature nor as an Aunt Sally. I intend it to represent the best that emotivism can do. An example will show what I am up to. Charles Stevenson produced in 1945 the fullest exposition of an emotivist theory that there has been (unless we include Allan Gibbard (1990), who was obviously deeply influenced by Stevenson; Gibbard calls himself a 'norm-expressivist'). Stevenson's book is made very confusing by his inclusion in his theory of subjectivist elements (drawn perhaps from Westermarck or from a misinterpretation of him). Thus his most famous analysis of moral judgements was of the form 'I approve of x; do so as well'. But the first half of this *analysans* sounds undeniably like a mere state-ment of psychological fact about the speaker, and so would be subjectivist, in the sense of Chapter 5. It would be a form of subject-ivist naturalism, and hence a form of descriptivism. And the addition of the imperative part of the *analysans*, 'Do so as well', does not do enough to remove the confusion.

There is evidence that many people were actually misled by this formulation. For example Ewing (1959) called his chapter criticizing non-descriptivism 'The New Subjectivism'. And Stevenson himself called his path-breaking earlier paper 'Moore's Arguments against Certain Forms of Ethical Naturalism' (1942), thus suggesting that what he, Stevenson, was defending was subjectivistic naturalism. So it was easy to be confused. We may note that when Stevenson wrote, Ayer, another famous emotivist, had already (1936: ch. 6) emphatic-ally dissociated himself from this kind of subjectivism, and cited arguments against it, drawn from Moore (1912: 57 ff.); so Stevenson had no excuse for this confusion. It would have been better if he had used only his second pattern of analysis, which has the merit of bringing out clearly the distinction between the two elements in the meaning of moral statements, the descriptive and the evaluative, the descriptive element being the standard of application of the moral words, and the evaluative being the expression of an attitude. By con-trast, the 'descriptive element' in 'I approve of x; do so as well' does *not* give a standard for the application of moral words; it is really an irrelevancy in the analysis, and should be replaced by an *expression*, not a *description*, of the speaker's attitude.

I want to avoid having to expose at tedious length what I think are simply mistakes in the emotivists' formulation of their theories, like this one. So I am going to give you a simplified version of emotivism which incorporates both the merits and the defects which I think are essential to it. What then is the element that the emotivists wanted to add to the analysis of the meaning of moral statements, so as to make them no longer purely descriptive? It had two aspects, which emotivists rightly distinguished. I will call these two aspects the *expressive* and the *causative*, and start by discussing the first of these.

6.2. Emotivists thought that when I make a moral statement, I am expressing an attitude of my own to an act, person, etc. Note carefully that expressing an attitude is different from *stating that* I have it. That is one way of stating the important difference between emotivism and subjectivism on which I have been laying so much stress. Earlier emotivists said, instead of 'attitude', 'feeling'; but 'attitude' is preferable, for reasons which Stevenson gave. I can say that as a matter of fact I have a certain attitude or feeling, without expressing it. Contrast two people, one of whom says, in a calm tone of voice, 'I am very angry with you for what you have done', and the other of whom says 'You blithering idiot!' The first is stating that he has a feeling (anger); the second is expressing it.

It is important to understand that there is nothing wrong, in one sense, with saying that when we make a moral statement we are expressing an attitude. For example, if I said 'Meat-eating is wrong' I should certainly be expressing an attitude to meat-eating. The trouble starts because of an unclarity or ambiguity in the word 'express'. Let us therefore look at this word more closely. The sense in which some emotivists were using it is indicated by Ayer's use of 'evince' as a synonym for it. If I evince anger, I am angry, and show it. So the impression we get is that the emotivists thought that when we make a moral statement, we have an attitude (for example of disapproval), and show it.

But even if this is a possible sense of 'express', it is certainly not the only one. Here is another. English expresses negation by the word 'not'. Russell and Whitehead expressed the same operation by the tilde sign, '∼'. Mathematicians express addition by the 'plus' sign (the sign shaped like a cross, '+'). Notice how odd it would be to say that mathematicians *evince* addition by this sign, or that English people *evince* negation by saying 'not'. It is not a question of having an attitude or feeling and showing it; it is, rather, a question of having something to say, and using this word in order to say it. Whenever we say anything, we are *expressing* our meaning, and expressing it correctly if we use the appropriate words. For this reason, philosophers often, when they want to talk about some word or phrase, refer to it as 'the *expression* "..."', followed by the word or phrase in quotation marks. Absolutely any word or phrase in the language is an expression in this sense.

I hope you will notice that the distinction between *expressing* and *stating that* survives into this different sense of 'express'. If I am writing something on a piece of paper, and someone asks me what I am writing, I may reply 'I am negating the statement that Stockholm is in Sweden'. In that case, if what I am writing is 'Stockholm is not in Sweden', what I say with my mouth is true; but what I am writing is false. So the negation I am *expressing* is false, but the *statement that* I am expressing it is true. So expressing cannot be the same as stating that.

Let us contrast the use of 'not' to express negation with the use, say, of 'Hell!' to express annoyance. There is one important difference that I should like you to notice. The word 'Hell!' can be used to express annoyance because in its literal sense 'Hell' is the name of a place, supposed to exist, which is an extremely nasty place to be in, where 'their worm dieth not and their fire is not quenched'. The use of 'Hell!' as an expression of anger is a metaphorical or transferred use. This is not so with 'not' as an expression of negation. In this respect expressions of moral attitudes resemble 'not' more than they do 'Hell!'. 'Not' expressing negation does not seem to be a transferred use; where could it be transferred from? It just is the word we have in English for negating. And similarly 'wrong' just is one of the words we have in English for expressing disapproval. The linguistic convention whereby the sound 'not' is the way we have in English for negating, or for expressing negation, is, in a sense, immediate, not derived or transferred; and the same is true of 'wrong' and disapproval.

It would be a good thing, therefore, if we put aside the associations of the word 'evince', and treated 'wrong' as a word for expressing disapproval in just the same way as we treat 'not' as a word for expressing negation. Both approval and negation are kinds of linguistic operation which have their appropriate expressions. But of course we have not said much about the meaning of 'wrong' when we have said that it is used to express disapproval. We need to go on to say what disapproval is.

It is obviously the opposite of approval; but what is approval? It, like disapproval, is primarily a linguistic operation. The *Oxford English Dictionary*, under 'approval', gives the meaning 'the action of declaring to be good'; and under 'approve' it gives the meaning 'pronounce to be good'. It says nothing there about feelings. But I must admit that it does define 'approbation' as 'approval expressed or felt'; so evidently there can *be* a feeling of approval. Still, the impression that we get from this dictionary is that approval is primarily a speech act, not a feeling or attitude. But to say this gets us no nearer to understanding *what* speech act.

Stevenson was not far wrong about this. He said, if I may summarize his view, that the attitude of approval is a disposition to *act* in the way approved of, and to encourage others to act in the same way. Thus, if moral words are expressions of approval or disapproval, the expressive aspect of their meaning joins up, as we might say, with the causative aspect. To have an attitude of approval is to be disposed to do a certain kind of act, and disposed to want or prescribe that others have the same disposition. This wanting is, I suppose, a feeling, so feeling has not got left out of the picture entirely; but it has assumed a subordinate role. So it looks as if we could best understand the expressive aspect of the meaning of moral statements by examining the causative aspect. This part of the emotive theory holds that it is a function of moral statements to *induce* feelings or attitudes or to *influence* conduct.

6.3. We can best discuss this causative function in connection with the assimilation of moral statements to imperatives—not because the meaning of imperatives lies in the function of inducing attitudes or getting people to do things. That, as we shall see, is a mistake. But since it was a mistake that emotivists generally made, the investigation of it will shed light on their theories. For if we can see what is wrong with saying that the meaning of *imperatives* is to be explained by saying that they are used to get people to do things, we shall be in a better position to see what is wrong with the very similar theory about moral statements.

It is extremely natural to think that one can explain the meaning of the imperative mood by saying that it is the mood one uses for getting people to do things. I have called this the 'verbal shove' theory of the meaning of imperatives (1.5, H 1996*b*). We find traces of views of this sort in many writers (e.g. A. Ross 1968: 68, see H 1969*b*; von Wright 1963: 149 f.; Castañeda 1974: 45, see H 1976*e*; Searle and Vanderveken 1985: 52). I have been controverting them throughout my career, but the mistake is very easy to make (H 1949, *LM* 12 ff., 1971*b*: *s.f.*). We often do use imperatives for getting people to do things. A little reflection, however, will show that we cannot explain their meaning in this way. For, first of all, sentences in other moods are used to get people to do things; and secondly, imperatives are sometimes used with other purposes than to get people to do the thing commanded or requested (the thing specified in the imperative). But meaning has to be something essential to the utterance of a sentence. If it is being used for some *other* purpose than shoving, *that* purpose cannot give its meaning, at least on this occasion of use. For example, if I say 'Keep quiet', what I am doing, on the 'verbal shove' theory, is trying to get the person addressed to keep quiet, and this is the meaning of my utterance. The view would be refuted if we found an instance of somebody saying 'Keep quiet', and meaning the normal thing by it, but not thereby trying to get the person or persons addressed to keep quiet.

Here is such an instance, which I remember first using in 1949. Two schoolmasters in old-fashioned boys' schools both say to their respective classes 'Keep quiet while I am out of the room'. One of them is really wanting and trying to get the boys to keep quiet. But the other, as soon as he has shut the door, puts his ear to the keyhole and, when the boys start to talk, as he hoped they would, flings open the door, gets out his stick and proceeds to indulge himself. Both of these schoolmasters meant the same by their words. It is not the case that the sadistic one really meant 'Talk while I am out of the room'. For if that were what he had meant, the boys would not have been disobeying him, and he would not have had an excuse for beating them. In order for his excuse to work, and for him not to get into trouble with the headmaster, he has to have told them to keep quiet. And this is indeed what has happened. The fact that by telling them to keep quiet he was (knowing boys to be naturally insubordinate) trying to get them, and wanting them, to talk, is strictly irrelevant to an account of the *meaning* of what he said.

A great many other examples could be given of imperative utterances which, although their meaning is clear, are not intended to *get* the people addressed to do the thing specified. Getting people to do the thing specified *is* a function which imperatives very frequently and typically have—and there is a reason, indeed, in their meaning why they should typically have this function; but this function cannot be used in explanation of their meaning. It is a *consequence* of their having the meaning that they have; the meaning explains this function, and not the other way round. I am here summarizing a long argument; what I have said is not conclusive as it stands, but I have no time to go at length into the matter. Perhaps it will help if I say a little in general about why this *sort* of explanation of meaning in terms of intended function will not do.

6.4　J. L. Austin (1962), as we have seen (1.5), distinguishes between three things that he calls the locutionary act, the illocutionary act, and the perlocutionary act. The distinction between the first two need not concern us now, even if it can be sustained, which I doubt (see H 1971c: 100 ff.). But the distinction between the first two taken together and the third is of great importance (see also Urmson 1968: ch. 11). To understand what is wrong with emotivism one has to grasp this distinction.

The perlocutionary effect of an utterance is what you are doing or trying to do *by* making it (*per locutionem*). It has, says Austin, to be distinguished from what you are doing *in* saying what you say (*in locutione*), the illocutionary act. And, even more, it has to be distinguished from the meaning of your utterance. For example, to revert to our sadistic schoolmaster: what he was doing *in* saying 'Keep quiet' was telling the boys to keep quiet; that was what his words meant. But what he was trying to do *by* saying it was to get them to talk, and so expose themselves to his eccentric *amours*. The reason why it is impossible in principle to explain meaning in terms of perlocutionary effect is that meaning, in the relevant sense, and illocutionary force if that is different, is something that belongs *by convention* to an utterance of a certain type made in a certain kind of situation. Thus the meaning of the utterance 'I promise to pay you a thousand kronor to-morrow', uttered in a normal situation (and not, for example, on the stage—1.3, H 1989*a*) is determined by the convention that the sounds 'I promise, etc.' are the sounds used in English for performing the speech act which we call 'promising to pay the addressee SwKr 1,000 on the following day'. We cannot give a series of sounds meaning, in the relevant sense of that word, without having a convention that that is how they are to be used—i.e. that that is the speech act that they express, or of whose expression they form part. Illocutionary force, if it is something different from meaning, is subject to the same condition: we cannot give to the sounds 'I promise, etc.' the power of carrying the illocutionary force of promising without having a convention that that is the speech act which they express.

But we could not, in principle, have a *convention* that a certain series of sounds was used for getting people to do things. We do, of course, have a convention that to utter a certain series of sounds is to *tell* someone to do a certain thing—that, for example, to utter the words 'Keep quiet' is to tell the people addressed to keep quiet—to perform the speech act of telling them. But telling them is not getting them, nor even (as we saw in the schoolmaster example) trying to get them. The reason why telling is a conventional activity, whereas getting or trying to get is not and cannot be, is that to tell somebody to do something *all* you have to do is follow the appropriate convention, and say 'Keep quiet' if you are speaking English, '*Chup rahō*' if you are speaking Hindi, and so on.

But in order to *get* someone to keep quiet, it is, perhaps, no use just performing speech acts according to the conventions. If you are going to get someone to keep quiet, he has to be disposed to keep quiet. One of the ways of so disposing him is to tell him to keep quiet; but the linguistic part of the procedure, the speech act, is over when you have told him—that is, when you have uttered the appropriate words in accordance with the linguistic conventions. You have done this, and given the words their *meaning*, whatever he subsequently does. The getting is an *effect* of the telling (an effect which may be produced by other means, such as doping or gagging him, or just frightening him speechless). When you are discussing meaning, it is the telling you are concerned with, and not the getting. Nor is it the trying to get which constitutes the telling. You can try to get him to keep quiet by telling him to; but these are different things. To give an analogy; I can try to loosen the top of the jam jar by heating it; but if one wanted to explain what heating *was*, one could not do it by saying that it was trying to loosen—partly because one could heat for many other purposes, and partly because there could be other ways by which one could try to loosen.

There is, of course, a reason why telling people to do things is normally a way of getting them to do them. This will become clearer if I say more positively what one is doing when one tells someone to do something. How, for example, do we distinguish what we are doing when we tell someone to keep quiet from what we are doing when we tell him that he is going as a matter of fact to keep quiet? What, in general, is the difference between typical imperatives and typical future indicatives or declaratives with the same content? I shall not be able to explain this at all fully; but perhaps I can make a start in this way. Suppose that I am speaking to an ideally complaisant person—a person who is disposed to accept, agree with, and in general assent to everything that I say. If I tell him that Jane is in the next room, he will believe me without question. If I tell him to shut the door, he will do it without question. The difference between the meanings of indicatives and imperatives can be brought out by saying that, in the case of an indicative, the complaisant (or, as I have sometimes called it, the accordant) response is *believing* whatever is said, whereas in the case of an imperative, the complaisant or accordant response is *doing* it.

People are not always complaisant; sometimes they are not disposed to accept or assent to what we say. If we know that they are countersuggestible, like the boys in the schoolmaster example, we may say one thing in the hope that they will believe, or do, the opposite. But normally we assume that our hearers are, for one reason or another, sufficiently complaisant to do or believe what we say. Otherwise co-operation would be difficult, if not impossible. So we do not normally ask or tell people to do things unless we think that they are, at least somewhat, disposed to do what we tell or ask them to;

and similarly we do not normally make statements to people unless we think that they are at least somewhat disposed to believe whatever we state to be the case. But, just as in the second case it would be a mistake to try to explain the meaning of the indicative mood by saying that it is the mood you use for trying to get people to believe things, so we must not step from the true explanation of the meaning of imperatives (namely, that an imperative is the kind of speech act, the complaisant or accordant response to which is to do, or become disposed to do, the thing specified) to the false notion that an imperative sentence is, essentially, an attempt to get someone to do the thing specified, and that this is an explanation of its meaning. Usually it is an attempt to get the thing done, but not essentially.

6.5. This is perhaps the best point at which to say something more about the expression 'pragmatics' which has caused so much confusion (1.5 f., H 1996*b*). If anybody uses it, one can be almost certain that he is going to confuse illocutionary with perlocutionary acts. 'Pragmatics' was one of a triad (the other two being 'syntactics' and 'semantics', which I have mentioned already). These three expressions were introduced by Charles Morris (1938; 1946: 216 f.) in a laudable attempt to bring some clarity into the general and very vague notion of 'meaning'. I do not want you to interpret me as saying that there is only one kind of meaning—only one sense of the word. There is even a sense of 'meaning' in which perlocutionary effect is part of meaning. All I am asking is that the different kinds of meaning should be carefully distinguished, and those which have to do with logic and rules for use separated from those which have not.

The trouble caused by the word 'pragmatics' (which predates Austin's distinction), comes out very clearly when people say, for example, that the meaning of imperatives is constituted by their pragmatics. Stevenson even said this sort of thing about moral statements. He called one of the main sections of his book (1945) 'Pragmatic Aspects of Meaning'. If he had meant by this something to do with illocutionary forces, I would have applauded him. But actually, because of the confusion caused by the word 'pragmatic', he seems to have argued as follows: moral statements (or ethical sentences as he called them) do not (at least do not primarily) express beliefs; they do not have meaning in the same way as ordinary descriptive statements have meaning. Therefore their meaning must be sought in their pragmatics. But because he failed to distinguish between illocutionary and perlocutionary acts, he plunged headlong into irrationalism. Meaning can be illocutionary, and therefore can be constrained by logical rules, even though it is not governed by truth conditions. The mistake was to think that because moral statements do not have their meaning determined wholly by their truth conditions, there can be no moral argument, or only very limited sorts of it. The word 'pragmatics' was, I think, mainly to blame for this mistake. The same confusion has been encouraged by some followers of Wittgenstein by indiscriminate bandying about of the expression 'the *use* of sentences', which could mean either their illocutionary or their perlocutionary use (1.5). Austin mentions this source of confusion too (1962: 100).

If it is a mistake to try to explain the meaning of *imperatives* in terms of their perlocutionary effect, it is obviously even more of a mistake to do this with moral statements. It is even more absurd to say that the essential function of moral statements—what gives them their meaning—is to *get* people to do things than it is to say this about imperatives. Opponents of emotivism have often pointed this out. If someone has just been drafted into the army and, having pacifist leanings, asks me whether he ought to obey the call-up and join the army, and I say to him 'Yes, you ought', I might not be *trying to get* him to join the army. He might think it an impertinence, or at least an unwarranted interference in a personal decision, to do any such thing as trying to get him to join the army. He asked for advice, not influence or inducement.

However, opponents of emotivism often, having pointed this out, go on to infer from it that moral judgements, since they are not attempts to get people to do things, cannot be anything like imperatives, because these *are* attempts to get people to do things. As we have seen (1.6), this has been used as an argument for a return to some kind of descriptivism, naturalistic or intuitionistic. But the argument has a false premiss. It is wrong to say that even imperatives are essentially attempts to get people to do things. Once this mistake about imperatives has been noticed, we are saved from a great many errors which have infected recent moral philosophy. The argument I have just mentioned, since the first of its premises is false, does not even prove that moral statements are not imperatives. It is not actually true that they are imperatives, and I have never said that they were (*LM* 1.1), although I have often been accused of doing this. My view is rather that they *share with* imperatives a very important feature, which I shall be calling *prescriptivity*. It is crucial, therefore, to see that to be prescriptive, even in the case of imperatives, is not the same as to have the essential function of getting people to do things. The theory that moral judgements are prescriptive is therefore not open to the attack I have just mentioned.

6.6. I want you to see how important this is. Perhaps I can help you see this by a bit of autobiography, which I hope you will pardon. When I started doing moral philosophy immediately after the Second World War, the emotivists were at the height of fashion, and the main controversy was between them and their opponents (H 1995*b*). The chief thing that seemed to divide the parties was that the emotivists denied that moral thinking could be a rational activity, whereas their opponents insisted that it could be. For this reason, emotivism was frowned on by all the good and great. Indeed, that was what made it so popular among the young. When I entered this scene, I was an opponent of emotivism, because I did want to show, if I could, that moral thinking could be rational. But I soon became convinced of the fallaciousness of the usual attacks on emotivism, which were all from a descriptivist standpoint. It became clear to me that what was needed was a non-descriptivist ethical theory which was at the same time *rationalist*. For I was quite certain that the emotivists were right in their non-descriptivism, but equally certain that they were wrong in thinking that there could not be rational argument about even the most fundamental moral questions.

The key to discovering a rationalist kind of non-descriptivism is this: to say that moral statements are prescriptive is to say something about their character as illocutionary acts; it is to say something about their illocutionary force (in Austin's term), and not about their perlocutionary effect. Both the emotivists and their opponents at that time thought otherwise. The emotivists had this wrong view about imperatives that I have been attacking; and they thought, consequently, that, in assimilating moral statements, as they did, to imperatives, they were saying something about their perlocutionary effect. But this would be quite useless as an explanation of their meaning, for the reasons I have given.

The opponents of emotivism shared, as I said, this false view about imperatives. They therefore thought that in order to show the rationality of moral thinking they had to reject what they loosely called 'the imperative theory' (this is one of the chapter-headings in Stephen Toulmin's early book *An Examination of the Place of Reason in Ethics* (1950), and by it he meant emotivism). And they included in this all forms of prescriptivism. So the whole controversy between the emotivists and their opponents was conducted on the wrong basis, and most of the confusions that have plagued moral philosophy ever since, right up to now, have been the effect of this mistake. The controversy was thought of as a battle between, on the one side, rationalist descriptivists, and, on the other, irrationalist non-descriptivists. It was taken for granted that rationalism was inseparable from descriptivism, and non-descriptivism from irrationalism. That explains why I have had such a hard time getting my views understood. For I have been maintaining a rationalist kind of non-descriptivism. And I can do that because of my avoidance of the mistake about imperatives that I have been pointing out.

If one thinks that imperatives, and prescriptive speech acts generally, have meaning in virtue of their use to get people to do things, then one is trying to explain their meaning in terms of their perlocutionary effect. But perlocutionary effect has nothing essentially to do with conventions or rules for the correct use of expressions. That indeed is why in principle it could not be used to explain meaning. But logic, as applied to a class of expressions, owes its existence and validity to these rules and conventions governing the use of expressions. For example, as we have seen (1.1 f.) the *modus ponens* form of argument ('If p then q; and p; so q') owes its validity to the rules governing the use of the expression 'if' and the other words in the sentences. But an explanation of the meanings of moral words in terms of perlocutionary effect cannot generate rules for their use, and therefore cannot generate a logic. A theory which relies on it is therefore bound to be irrationalist. However, once we see that the correct explanation of the meanings of both moral words and imperatives is in terms of their illocutionary force, not their perlocutionary effect, we see, also, that it is possible to say that moral statements and imperatives are different varieties of the kind of speech act called prescribing, and that, since their meaning can be thus characterized in terms of their illocutionary force, it *does* determine rules for their use, and thus generates a logic. So there can be rational moral argument even though moral judgements are prescriptive.

I hope I have now convinced you that, since imperatives can be governed by logical rules arising out of their meaning and illocutionary force, it would be possible to be even an imperativist in ethical theory (that is, to assimilate moral statements completely to ordinary imperatives) without being an irrationalist. I am not, and never have been, an imperativist, because I think that moral statements share only one feature with imperatives, their prescriptivity, and have other features which they do not share with imperatives, and which make them more like indicatives (in particular the fact that they can be true or false and have truth conditions). But since this one feature, prescriptivity, stops us calling moral statements *purely* descriptive, it is very important to see that they can have it, without making rational argument about moral questions impossible. I have tried to show in my books how such arguments can be conducted, and I will summarize my view on this in Chapter 7.

6.7. I am now in a position to complete the main framework of my taxonomy of ethical theories, though I shall deliberately leave a corner of it open (5.8). I divided ethical theories into the species descriptivist and non-descriptivist, the *differentia* being that the former affirmed, and the latter denied, that the meaning of moral statements is wholly determined, apart from syntactical features, by their truth conditions. I then divided descriptivist theories into naturalism, in its objectivist and subjectivist varieties, and intuitionism, and showed that all these forms of descriptivism are bound to collapse in one way or another into relativism, which I showed to be unacceptable. I then turned to non-descriptivist theories, and considered the earliest variety of these, emotivism. I found in this some virtues but one serious fault, that it could find no place for rational moral argument about fundamental moral questions. This gives us the *differentia* which divides non-descriptivism into its two main varieties. The variety that I have discussed so far, emotivism, is an irrationalist sort of non-descriptivism. I shall go on in Chapter 7 to set out a rationalist sort of non-descriptivism, which will also yield a *kind*, though not a descriptivist kind, of objectivity for moral statements. For if moral thinking can be shown to be rational, then we can expect rational thinkers to agree in their moral opinions once they are in possession of the facts and think clearly. So I wish to divide non-descriptivism into its rationalist and irrationalist varieties. I do not claim that my taxonomy of non-descriptivism is complete. That is, there may be (I am sure that there are) further subdivisions of these two kinds of non-descriptivism. In the case of descriptivism, I showed, I hope, that all its possible varieties were inadequate. In the case of non-descriptivism I have not claimed so much. We shall in Chapter 7 look at a variety of rationalist non-descriptivism which I think is the most adequate ethical theory so far devised. But there may be other varieties of rationalist non-descriptivism which will do better. I am not trying to close the door to new and improved theories, but shall, as I said, leave a corner open. But I am quite sure that the only ones with any promise will have their place on the non-descriptivist side of the taxonomy, and in its rationalist segment.

Even in the case of emotivism it is possible that improvements could be suggested which make it no longer irrationalist. For example, as we have seen, Allan Gibbard, calls himself a norm-expressivist (which sounds very Stevensonian), and goes on in the latter part of his excellent book (1990) to claim that in his theory a kind of objectivity can be achieved in moral statements. His title is significant: *Wise Choices, Apt Feelings*. Although his language often suggests that he is an emotivist, we should probably not classify him as an irrationalist. But he is without doubt a non-descriptivist, and has some telling criticisms of recent descriptivists such as John McDowell. So perhaps we should classify him as a rationalist non-descriptivist like me. I shall not have time in this book to examine his complex theory in detail; but I like to think of him as being in the same camp as myself, and look on its publication as a sign that the descriptivist tide may have turned.

6.8. What I am going on to do in the rest of this chapter is to state, as briefly as I can, what I think are the essential features that an ethical theory has to have if it is to be adequate; that is, the features of moral language and its logic, as we have them, which a theory must do justice to if it is to be tenable. This will provide us with a sort of sieve through which we can put any ethical theory; if it fails to pass through the sieve because it does not do justice to any one of these features, it has to be rejected. I shall then make amends by drawing attention to the *good* points of each of the theories I have discussed (the features of moral thought and language to which it does do justice). Then we shall be in a position to try to draw together these good features into one theory, while rejecting the bad points. And that is what I hope to do. Thus my theory will be an eclectic one in a good sense (H 1994*b*).

There are, I think, six features of moral statements that would make me want to reject any theory that failed to do justice to them. Most of them I have mentioned already. I have given my sieve to catch inadequate ethical theories in the table on p. 42. It shows with a cross which of the theories, in my view, fail to satisfy which requirements. (1) First of all, no ethical theory—that is, no account of the meaning of the moral words and the logic of moral argument which that brings with it—can do anything for actual moral arguments unless it can be accepted by both parties to the arguments. This means that it is always fatal to try to smuggle moral opinions of substance into one's ethical theory in the guise of mere definitions or explanations of meaning, as in effect the objectivistic naturalists do. If one party to the argument does not like the conclusions to which he is thereby forced, he will reject the theory, and we will be back where we started. I shall call this requirement the requirement of *neutrality*. I think that objectivistic naturalism is the only theory, of those examined, which fails this test. It fails it because an objectivist account of the truth conditions of moral statements which is at the same time naturalist (that is, which formulates them in terms of non-moral properties) is bound to introduce substantial moral stipulations into the theory; and if anybody does not like the stipulations he will reject the theory.

(2) Secondly, no ethical theory is going to be of any use for practice if it leads only to moral conclusions of what I shall call the 'So what?' sort. By this I mean that if, at the end of a moral argument, one of the disputants is forced to agree to a moral conclusion, but can then say 'Yes, it would be wrong to do that; so what?', then the system of moral argument is a fraud. I give an example of such a failure in *MT* 4.3. This requirement I shall call the requirement of *practicality*. It is failed by all forms of descriptivism, because they leave out the prescriptive element in the meaning of moral statements.

(3) Next, an account of the meanings of moral words has to be such that the moral disagreements that we find going on really are disagreements. We saw that this requirement was not met by the theory called subjectivistic naturalism. According to it, if I call an act wrong and you call it not wrong, we are stating, respectively, that I have a certain feeling or attitude and that you have a certain opposite feeling or attitude; and we are therefore not saying two things which are incompatible with each other. I shall call this the *incompatibility*-requirement. So far as I can see, it is failed only by subjectivistic naturalism, though if, as I have claimed, there is no real difference between intuitionism and subjectivism, intuitionism fails it too. But the intuitionists certainly did not think they failed it; they thought that there could be real disagreement about whether an act possessed or did not possess the objective moral property of wrongness. So I will allow them to pass this requirement. I think that it was Stevenson's big contribution to show, in his misnamed article 'Moore's Arguments against Certain Forms of Ethical Naturalism' (1942) that non-descriptivist theories can satisfy this requirement.

I must add that, as I said in 4.3, objectivistic naturalism *would* fail this requirement if, in order to escape the argument I there advanced against it, its proponents took refuge in saying that different cultures who have different mores are using the moral words in different senses. There would then really be no disagreement between the cultures other than a merely verbal one.

(4) Fourthly, and closely connected with the incompatibility requirement (indeed, it is a kind of generalization of it), there must be a place in the theory for logical relations between moral statements. The incompatibility of the statement that an act is wrong with the statement that it is not wrong is an example of a logical relation. But it is not the only sort of logical relation that is required. Perhaps all logical relations are reducible to relations of incompatibility. For example, the relation that we call entailment or deducibility can be so reduced: a proposition *p* entails another proposition *q* if and only if *p* is incompatible with not-*q*. Any ethical theory has to admit of logical relations of the following sort: that the two propositions that it is always wrong to tell lies, and that to say so-and-so would be to tell a lie, are conjointly incompatible with the proposition that it would not be wrong to say so-and-so. I am not going at the moment to ask *what* logical relations hold between moral propositions, or between them and other propositions; all I insist on is that *some* should. I say this not only because without such logical relations moral argument would be impossible (that I am coming to in a moment), but because it is quite evident to anyone who knows the language that we do use words in such a way that *some* moral statements are incompatible with at least some other moral statements. Let us call this the requirement of *logicality*. As we saw, it is not fully satisfied by various forms of the emotive theory, though some of them allow subsumptive arguments in moral thinking (I shall return to this point shortly).

Reverting for a moment to requirement (2), that of practicality: having accepted the requirement of logicality, we can now put the requirement of practicality in a somewhat clearer and more convenient form by saying that at least some moral statements have to have logical relations with *prescriptive* speech acts of some sort (e.g. imperatives). I shall not, however, insist for the moment on this; the looser way I put it earlier will suffice.

(5) If we put together requirements (3) and (4) (incompatibility and

logicality) we are led to a further requirement. This is that our ethical theory should do something to resolve moral disagreements by the use of argument. I deliberately do not say that it should make it possible to resolve *all* moral disagreements by argument. If we look at what goes on in moral arguments, we see (if my experience is any guide) that some disagreements are resolved by argument and some are not. An ethical theory could be wrong in two ways: either by making it impossible to reach agreement by argument in cases where it is possible, or by claiming that it is possible to prove things in moral argument where it is not possible. We must avoid both of these opposite errors. You may remember that in *FR* 8.1 f. I said that the form of argument I was advocating there did not enable us to argue about ideals where no other people's interests are affected; if I was right, this may be an example of a matter which *cannot* be settled by argument. On the other hand, I have argued that where other people's interests *are* affected, cogent arguments about moral questions are available (*MT* pt. 2, H 1993*g*). So let us call our moderate requirement, that the theory should do *something* to resolve moral disagreements by the use of argument, the *arguability* requirement.

A theory which fails to satisfy the requirement of logicality cannot satisfy that of arguability, if by 'argument' we mean 'logical argument'. Some emotivists (Ayer for example, and Stevenson) do allow there to be limited forms of argument about moral questions; but they are limited to the subsumption of particular moral statements under more general ones, and in any case it is not clear whether this is for Stevenson a matter of logical derivation or merely of causing attitudes to change by invoking more general attitudes. I think that we do allow there to be arguments about moral questions which are more ambitious than this—arguments which can reach a conclusion even between people who do not share *any* initial substantial moral opinions; indeed, I shall be showing in Chapter 7 how this can be done.

As is clear from what I said in Chapter 5 about what happens when intuitions disagree, intuitionism does not satisfy the arguability requirement. In fact, intuitionists are in no better position than emotivists when it comes to argument. The disputants can do no more than oppose their intuitions to one another. There can be subsumption of particular moral statements under more general ones; but even emotivists can do that. Naturalism fails this test too, because it fails to satisfy the neutrality requirement; as I said, if the naturalist proposes an account of the meaning of a moral word which he thinks will settle the dispute between two parties, the party that is defeated will at once reject the naturalist's account. The naturalist has no neutral standpoint from which to adjudicate between them.

6.9. So then, all the theories we have so far discussed fail to meet one or other of these five requirements. I wish to add to these a sixth requirement. This is of a somewhat different character to the others, being a practical rather than a theoretical requirement.

(6) An adequate ethical theory has to make it possible for moral discourse and moral thought in general to fulfil the purpose that they have in society. This is to enable those in society who disagree about what they should do, especially in matters which affect their divergent interests, to reach agreement by rational discussion. I shall call this requirement, that morality and the moral language should be enabled by our ethical theory to preserve their function of reconciling conflicting interests, the *conciliation* requirement.

Moral language, whose meaning ethics tries to elucidate, is one of the most remarkable inventions of the human race, comparable at least with mathematical language. It is not such an ancient invention as is sometimes thought. Perhaps it is comparable with mathematical language in this respect too, that we can watch its development during the course of recorded history. Just as the ancient Greeks had arithmetic and Euclidean geometry and their languages, but did not have the calculus and its language, so you may, if you look carefully at how people talked at various times in history, see that the Greeks did not have a moral language as fully developed as ours, and that our present-day moral language has features which were not *fully* developed (though of course there were more primitive forms of them) until perhaps the time of Kant or even of Mill.

I am not agreeing here with those who think that a mere alteration in mores (in the moral principles generally accepted) involves a change in the meanings of the moral words. This, as I have said, is a mistake to which descriptivists are prone, and it leads to relativism. People can change their moral opinions, even quite radically, without changing the meaning, apart from the descriptive meaning, of the moral words that they use. I gave as an example the Christian precept that we should love our enemies; to accept this is to alter our moral convictions radically, but it does not entail a shift in the meaning of 'should'. But all the same the structure and logic of moral language does change with time; for example, the universalizability of moral statements, which is now, I am sure, a logical feature of the moral words, was not always so. Probably it has become so in the course of history as a result of Christian teaching, and the work of philosophers like Kant. It is a frequent phenomenon in language that sentences which used to express synthetic statements change their meaning, so that the statements they express become analytic. For example, the sentence 'water is composed of two parts of hydrogen and one of oxygen' once expressed a synthetic discovery; but now one (but only one) of the senses of 'water' is *defined* by dictionaries in that way, thus making the statement that water is H_2O, in the new sense of the word 'water', analytically true (H 1984*b*, 1996*d*). This phenomenon was well documented by von Wright (1941: ch. 3).

The function of this remarkable language, the language of morals, is to help us sort out certain difficulties which are bound to arise when people live in communities, and in which, therefore, conflicts of interest inevitably occur. People have desires and needs which cannot all be realized because they conflict with the desires and needs of other people. Morality and the moral language are an invention for dealing with this situation. I used the word 'invention' in this context long before John Mackie used it in the title of his very good book *Ethics: Inventing Right and Wrong* (1977); but I agree with him that it is an invention, though we disagree about some other things.

It might be asked why, if moral language has these wonderful properties, it has not enabled us already to sort out all our moral disagreements. The answer is twofold. First, many of these disagreements are rooted in disagreements about the facts, which in any at all intractable moral problem are bound to be extremely complex and hard to establish. But, more importantly, not many people are able to think clearly about moral questions with an understanding of the words they are using. They may therefore be expected to get confused, and indeed examples of such confusions can be observed by anybody who reads the newspapers, especially their correspondence columns. And in any case many people do not think morally at all, but at most shmorally.

If, as I have claimed, the language in its fully developed form is a recent growth, these failings are even easier to understand. And the prevalence of descriptivism and other philosophical errors, which are bound to some extent to infect public discussions, does not help. I am sure that if we had better moral philosophy, we should have less public perplexity and confusion about moral questions. But I am not at all hopeful that this will actually happen; there are too many bad moral philosophers throwing dust in our eyes, and all too few good ones clarifying the issues.

Unlike the others, the conciliation requirement is more of a practical requirement than a logical one, as I said; and this is important, because if I can show that the theory I am going to propose meets it in practice, that will do. It will not be an objection to the theory if it can be argued that there logically could be communities in which the requirement would not be satisfied.

It is, I think obvious that none of the theories I have so far considered can satisfy this requirement, because they all fell down on one or other of the requirements I have listed; and in particular all of them failed to satisfy the arguability requirement. Conciliation through moral reasoning will clearly be impossible between people who do not know how to argue morally.

So then we have these six requirements for an adequate ethical theory. They are only the ones which seem to me the most important: people might bring forward other requirements and think them more important. In this connection I might mention the so-called publicity requirement by which Rawls and others set store. It is not a requirement for an ethical theory (Rawls does not have an ethical theory in my sense), but rather a requirement for a substantial moral principle, namely that it could be openly avowed without defeating its object. I am not sure that this *is* a requirement for a moral principle; but since we are doing ethical theory not 'moral theory' in Rawls's sense I shall not discuss it. I think that the ethical theory I am going to put before you satisfies all my six requirements, and all other requirements that I am aware of—which is not to say that it is the last word in ethical theories, because, as always, problems remain. But I think it is the most adequate ethical theory I have come across so far.

7

RATIONALISM

7.1. Up to now this part of my book has been mostly devoted to fault-finding. I am next going to make amends by telling you what I think are the virtues of the theories I have discussed. This is not just in order to be fair, nor just in order to show my good nature. I have two ulterior motives. The first is self-protective. The best way of protecting one's own theory is to incorporate into it all the *truths* that upholders of rival theories insist on (H 1994*b*). Then they are less likely to attack one, and will not be successful if they do. The second is constructive. If, as I believe, nearly all ethical theories contain some elements of truth, the best way of constructing a viable one is to pick out the true elements in each and build them into one's own theory. I advise all those who want to make a career in philosophy to do this. A good politician tries to steal his enemies' clothes, and a good philosopher does the same. He looks carefully at all the theories that have been put forward and asks himself what is true in each of them; if he can then lay hold on these truths and avoid the errors which there are also likely to be, he will have a defensible theory. *Veritati omnia consentiunt.* This is of course difficult, because in most theories the truths are closely meshed with the errors, and it is hard to take them apart. The adherents of the theories, who have not seen that the truths do not entail the errors, will always resist this treatment. But if one can achieve this kind of benign eclecticism, one will be a successful philosopher.

I will start with the truths in objectivistic naturalism. I have discussed them in *MT* ch. 4, so I can be brief. The first is that it grasps the essential point of ethical theory, which is, by examining the language of morals, the moral concepts and their logic, to show how we can reason correctly about moral questions. So the objectivistic naturalist's project is the right one, though he executes it badly. But not all that badly. There is another very important truth he has got hold of. He has grasped that moral statements are made about actions for *reasons*, namely that the actions have certain non-moral properties. An act was wrong, for example, *because* it was an act of hurting somebody for fun. This property of moral statements, their supervenience on non-moral statements, is crucial to an understanding of them. But the objectivistic naturalist has misunderstood the nature of the 'because'. He mistakes supervenience for entailment, and thus makes into analytically true statements what are really substantial moral principles. That it is wrong to hurt people for fun is not an analytic statement. But still the act is wrong *because* it was that sort of act. So the objectivistic naturalist has hit on, though he has not fully understood, the supervenience or consequentiality of moral properties, and thus is on the track of the universalizability of moral statements which lies at its root (on supervenience see 1.7, H 1984*b*, 1996*d*). This important feature of moral statements we have to incorporate into our own theory.

Next the subjectivistic naturalists. They let slip the important truth I have just found in objectivistic naturalism. For all that they say, it is a sufficient reason for saying that an act is wrong that you disapprove of it; it does not have to be wrong because of anything about it except that. But nevertheless the subjectivist has got hold of an important truth, namely that something in the attitudes of the speaker goes into the making of a moral statement. Subjectivists have not understood very well what this something is; the emotivists understood it better, and the prescriptivists better still; but subjectivism was a promising beginning.

The intuitionists also had hold of some important truths, both negative and positive. They insisted, against the naturalists, on the non-analyticity of moral principles, while upholding also their consequentiality. The expression 'consequential property' comes, I believe, from the intuitionists, as does the expression 'supervenience', though I have not been able to locate it in their writings. Although the intuitionists mistook condemning an action for perceiving a property of wrongness in it, they were right about many of the logical properties of moral statements. They rightly insisted that 'I ought' contradicts 'I ought not', and that therefore it was impossible consistently to agree with both. There was also another thing right about them which I shall not be able to explain until later, when I have discussed the two levels of moral thinking, the intuitive and the critical (7.8). Intuition has an important place in moral thinking, though it is not an ultimate court of appeal as the intuitionists think. And most of what they say is correct about the intuitive level of moral thinking.

The emotivists, as I have said, took a very important step forward in ethical theory when they rejected descriptivism. Although they made a serious error in trying to explain what moral statements do, they were clear that they do not just describe the world. Moral statements do more than this, but it was left to others to explain what this more was.

7.2. Taking stock, therefore, of our present position, we have the following truths gleaned from the theories so far considered which have to be incorporated into a more adequate theory. First, it must show, by an examination of the meanings and logic of moral words, how we can reason about moral questions. The place of logic in the theory will be crucial, for without it there can be no reasoning. Secondly, it must show how we can make moral statements *because* of the non-moral properties of the actions, etc. that we are speaking about. In other words, it must do justice to the consequentiality or supervenience of moral properties, which is linked to the universalizability of moral statements. Thirdly, it must do justice to the fact that in making a moral statement the speaker is himself contributing something. Morality is not a passive perception of the world. The subjectivists were half right about this, but because they were still descriptivists they thought that, since in a moral statement one is not describing the world, one must be describing oneself. Lastly, while rejecting descriptivism like the emotivists, and insisting that there is something extra to the making of a moral statement beyond the describing of an action or a person in accordance with truth conditions, an adequate ethical theory must give an account of this extra ingredient in moral statements which is consistent with their being subject to logical control.

This extra ingredient is the prescriptivity of moral statements, and the realization that it does not conflict with their logicality. That is what I have been after ever since I started doing moral philosophy, and I still think it is the most important thing we have to understand if we want to make sense of moral thinking and moral argument. I am going in what follows to show why it is prescriptive logic, if I may so call it, that makes rationality in moral thinking possible, and not, or at least not only, the fact that moral statements have truth conditions. They *have* truth conditions, indeed, but if those were all we had to rely on, we could not escape relativism. It is the fact that when we are adopting a moral principle we are *prescribing* that gives rational moral argument its teeth (H 1996*c*). Because, as I have said, the prescriptivity of moral statements, unlike their descriptive meanings, can be a culturally invariant element in them, it enables them to be used in rational discussion *between* cultures. I will now try to explain this more clearly.

We saw earlier that the truth conditions of a moral statement are inevitably relative to a culture and its mores and language. If a certain culture accepts certain moral principles, they will be enshrined in both its language and its moral education, and any theory which looks for truth conditions in language or in intuition will be trapped inside the culture. What is needed is a way of criticizing the moral principles of a culture: a way of discussing in rational argument whether we should or should not accept those principles. Many cultures have moral principles that we ought to reject; but the members of those cultures, if they are descriptivists, will have no reason to reject them.

It is the requirement to *prescribe* in accordance with these principles which makes us reject some of them. Here I am following Kant (8.6 f.). I suppose most people who study Kant, being themselves descriptivists like Prichard and Ross, read their own prejudices into Kant and do not notice that he is not himself a descriptivist. In the most famous of his formulations of his Categorical Imperative, he says that we are so to act that we can *will* the maxim of our action to become a universal law. The will is a prescriptive, not a descriptive faculty. In this it is like Aristotle's *phronēsis*. Aristotle himself is half a prescriptivist (H 1992*e*: ii. 1304; 1998*a*). He contrasts *phronēsis*, or practical wisdom, with *synesis* or understanding, and says that the former is *epitātikē* (which actually *means* 'prescriptive') but the latter is *krītikē monon*—it only judges, not prescribes. The distinction comes from Plato's *Statesman* (260b). Both Plato and Aristotle were in part, like Kant and Mill, prescriptivists, following Socrates in this (H 1998a). This comes out also in the fact that in Aristotle's practical syllogism the conclusion is an action or prescription for action. If it is, and if the syllogism is valid, then one of the premisses has to be prescriptive, and this premiss is obviously the first, which is a moral or other normative statement. So Aristotle realized that normative statements are prescriptions. It also comes out when, at the very beginning of the *Nicomachean Ethics*, he says that the good is what all things seek; in this too he is following Plato. But Plato's and Aristotle's prescriptivism was heavily overlaid with descriptivist elements; so most commentators have not noticed it.

7.3. This is obviously not the place to expound Plato or Aristotle in detail. I will, however, say a little more about Kant, additional to what I say in 8.2 ff., because he gives us some important clues on how to *discipline* moral thinking, even though it is prescriptive. Descriptivists think they can discipline it by insisting that it obey truth conditions; but as we have seen this only lands them in relativism. Kant speaks very seldom, if ever, about the truth or the truth conditions of moral statements, or about moral facts. He speaks about what we can *will* as a universal *law*.

The will, as I said, is a prescriptive faculty. The nature of the discipline imposed on it by the Categorical Imperative will be revealed if we can understand what Kant meant by '*can* will'. What sort of possibility is he thinking of? Unfortunately he is not entirely consistent on this, and he has at least two accounts of the matter, one of which does not help much. This is the account which says that the restriction on the will is simply that its maxims have to be logically consistent, in the sense that to say that the maxims had been obeyed would not involve a self-contradiction. As many commentators have pointed out, there are some very wicked maxims that logically could be obeyed, so that this discipline for moral thinking is inadequate. It will not even do to say that the *universalized form* of a maxim has to be free of contradiction. For some bad maxims could slip through even this net. For example, I can without contradiction will that everybody should seek his own selfish advantage and pay no attention to the needs of others; and I think that some people actually follow this maxim in their actions, so it is not self-contradictory to say that such a maxim has been obeyed. Of course it goes without saying that we have to avoid contradiction in our maxims; but that is not enough to keep us on the moral rails.

I conclude that the 'can' in the Categorical Imperative is not just a logical 'can'. Is it then a psychological 'can'? It is said that there are also some very bad maxims that some people could bring themselves, psychologically speaking, to will to be universal laws, at any rate if their circumstances were such that they would never be the victims of the actions prescribed. Could not a hard-hearted person, who could be confident that he would never be in the position of his victim, will to go on torturing him for fun? Something more seems to be needed than logical, and than psychological, possibility.

At this point I am going to suggest my own solution (already summarized in 1.8) to this problem. I think I have found it in Kant, though it is not the only possible interpretation of his text, and indeed different passages can be interpreted in different ways. This is no place for detailed exegesis of Kant, any more than of Aristotle or Plato. I return to Kant in Chapter 8. But what I think he *ought* to have said is this. If we have to will our maxims as universal laws, we have to will that they should be observed in all situations resembling one another in the universal features specified in the maxim. These features will include features of the psychological states of the people in the situations. For example, if we are speaking of victims of torture, the fact that they badly want the torture to stop is a feature of their psychological states, and therefore of their situations. We have then to will that our maxims should be observed whatever individuals were in these states, even ourselves. This helps to explain the 'can' in the Categorical Imperative.

Can I will that if I were being tortured the torturer should go on torturing me? Let us suppose that no other considerations come into my thinking. For example, it is not the case that I think I deserve

punishment, or think I should deserve it if I were in that situation—
one in which, say, I have committed a heinous crime. Suppose it just
is the case that the torturer *enjoys* torturing me. I do not think that I
can will this. The reason is not just psychological impossibility. For I
suppose that one might find somebody who, empirically speaking, did
will that he should himself go on being tortured if he were ever in
that situation. I am not speaking of masochists; they are supposed to
want to be tortured, which is not the position of the victim in our
example. I dare say I might want to be tortured just to see what it was
like; but that is not our present case, because the torture has already
started and I am asking whether I can will that if I were being tortured the torturer should go on torturing me. I repeat: I do not think I
can will this. It is not just that I *happen* not to like being tortured.
Torture is by definition a cause of suffering; if it is not a cause of suffering it is not torture. And suffering is something that by definition
the sufferer wants to stop; if he does not want it to stop (other things
being equal, of course) it is not suffering. So at any rate *at the time* the
sufferer cannot will that the torture should go on, other things being
equal.

But can I *in advance*, and for a hypothetical situation, will that the
torture should go on? This hangs on a tricky question about personal
identity (1.8). I am inclined to the view that, if I will that the torture
should go on in the hypothetical situation, I am not thinking of the
victim as *myself*. As I said in *MT*, there are several different criteria of
personal identity which in nearly all cases coincide, so that no problem arises; they come apart in philosophers' examples, and sometimes in rare brain disorders, and then we do not know what to say.
One of these features (though not exactly a *criterion*) of personal
identity is this: I have, if I am thinking of a possible future person as
myself, to identify with him (or her) to the extent of preferring that
his preferences should be satisfied. That is, it is part of the concept of
personal identity that each person has an interest in his *own* future. If
someone has lost interest in his own future, he is to that extent not
thinking of the future person as *himself*.

From this I conclude that unless I will, now, that the torture should
not go on in the hypothetical situation, I am not thinking of the tor-

ture victim as *me*. To this add the idea, put forward in detail in *MT*, that unless I fully represent to myself what it is like for *me* to be in that situation, I am not in full possession of the facts about the situation. The argument can then get going. It follows that *if* I am in full possession of the facts about the situation (and of course, if I am not, I can be faulted for ignorance of the facts), then I shall not be able to will that the torture go on in the hypothetical case in which I am the victim. This is the first part of the explanation of the 'can' as it figures in my version of Kant's Categorical Imperative. I cannot will that *I* should be treated like that if I were the victim. But this does not take us the whole way. True, I will that *I* should not go on being tortured if I were in that situation. But this says nothing about what I can or cannot will should be done to the other person who is actually the victim. For all that we have said so far I can will that *he* should go on being tortured.

7.4. I have been merely summarizing, so far, the argument of *MT* ch. 5. My object is twofold: first, to show the absolutely crucial part that prescriptivity plays in the entire argument; and secondly, to relate my own argument to Kant's. I hope you will have noticed that a descriptivist, even if he believed in universalizability, as many descriptivists do, could not use the argument I have been using so far. The question 'Can I *will?*' has been central; and willing is a kind of prescribing. It does not enter into the descriptivist's vocabulary. For me, as for Kant, the point is not that a certain kind of action cannot be *described*, or even described as universally occurring, without self-contradiction, but that it cannot be willed or prescribed universally.

But we have not yet brought universalizability into the argument. Many people who have read *MT* carelessly have supposed that it plays an essential part in the argument of *MT* ch. 5. This is not so. That chapter establishes something about prescriptivity, not about universalizability. Universalizability only enters essentially into the argument in *MT* ch. 6. But if the ground had not been prepared in *MT* ch. 5 by establishing the thesis that there is something that we cannot *prescribe*, namely that we ourselves should be tortured in the hypothetical situation (indeed something that we shall necessarily prescribe, namely that we ourselves should *not* be tortured), the argument from universalizability in *MT* ch. 6 would get no grip. Descriptivists therefore could not deploy it. You will now, I hope, see the tactics of my general argument. In Chapters 4 and 5 I showed that descriptivism of all sorts collapsed into relativism and could not yield objectivity in moral statements. Then I expressed the hope that a non-descriptivist theory could yield this objectivity. By 'objectivity' I mean not 'correspondence with the facts' or anything like that. I leave all that to the descriptivists; it is a dead end. I mean, rather, by 'object-ive', 'such as any rational thinker in possession of the non-moral facts must agree to'. If we could show that some moral statements have this property, I should be content. In this sense, though not in the sense that Mackie denied the possibility of them, I shall maintain that there can be objective *prescriptions* (H 1993*g*).

If we add to the foregoing argument the requirement to universal-ize our prescriptions, the argument can be completed. It will be obvi-ous to you how it will go. If I cannot will that *I* should be treated in that way in that situation, then I cannot will universally that *whoever* is in that situation should be treated in that way. So, if I am going to make a moral statement about the situation, and moral statements are universal prescriptions, then here is one that I cannot make. I can of course assent to *singular* prescriptions: I can *want* to go on tortur-ing my victim; but I cannot say that I ought to.

Here, as you will realize, I should have to deal with the position of the amoralist who will not make any moral statements at all about the situation; but I have discussed him enough in *MT* 10.7 ff., H 1989*d*, and 1996*e*. I have also discussed (in 5.8) the position of the shmoralist. Leaving them aside, and confining our attention to those who want to make some moral statement about the situation, we have at least ruled out one, namely that I ought to go on with the tor-ture. This is a conclusion with which all rational thinkers must agree, that is, an objective conclusion.

In what I have just been saying there lies the answer to two rather weak arguments that one often comes across. They are arguments against the kind of theory I am putting forward. Sometimes it is said that if all that is required is that we should prescribe some maxim universally, this does not stop us advocating maxims which are tailored to our own interest; and it is also said, more generally, that it does not stop us advocating maxims that we all find outrageous.

An example of the first kind of argument is this: suppose someone says that he prescribes universally that people with six fingers on one hand should be given special privileges, and that he has six fingers on one hand. His maxim is formally impeccable; it is a universal prescription in the fullest sense of 'universal'. The maxim is not in itself contradictory; so, if we took the line of some interpreters of Kant, we could not fault it. But the question is, 'Can he adopt this maxim if he is in full cognizance of the facts, which he can only be if he has fully represented to himself the situations of those who would be adversely affected by his adoption of this maxim?' As we have seen, full representation of another's situation involves forming preferences as to what should happen to oneself, were one in that situation; and this, combined with the requirement to universalize one's maxims, will cause him to reject his proposed maxim. For he will form preferences that, were he in the positions of all those who will suffer if he gets his privileges, the privileges should be withdrawn. And these preferences are incompatible with the retention of his maxim.

Here is an example of the second kind of argument, which is very similar. It is said that the prescription to keep all black people in subjection is formally universal, and internally consistent, and so is not ruled out by the Categorical Imperative. But the point is: can somebody who has fully represented to himself the situation of black people who are kept in subjection go on willing that they should be so treated? For if he has fully represented this to himself, he will have formed a preference that he should not be so treated if he is a black person; and this is inconsistent with the universal form of the proposed maxim. There is of course the problem of the fanatical blackhater who is prepared to prescribe that the maxim should be followed even if he himself were a black person. I have discussed the case of this fanatic at length in my books (e.g. *MT* 10.3), and I think I have shown that my theory can deal with him; but there is no time now to go into that problem. At any rate the Kantian move can be used in arguments with ordinary non-fanatical people.

7.5. I have perhaps taken things in the wrong order by telling you how one could argue on the basis of the theory I propose without first telling you what the theory is, except in so far as I said it was an adaptation of Kant's Categorical Imperative. Let me now, therefore, try to formulate the theory more clearly. The first thing I need to say about it is that it gives a completely *formal* account of the meanings of the moral words. By this I mean that it defines them purely on the basis of their logical properties. Contrast naturalism, which defines them or explains their meaning in terms of substantial non-moral properties. Let us take 'ought' as an example. 'Ought', I want to say, *is* a logical word. It is a deontic modal operator. Its logical properties and function are closely analogous to those of the other modal operators like 'it is necessary that'. The difference is that, whereas the other modal operators govern descriptive statements, 'ought' governs prescriptions (*MT* 1.6). 'Ought'-statements entail imperatives with the same content, just as sentences beginning 'It is necessary that . . .' entail indicative statements with the same content. So we could summarize my account of 'ought' by saying that it is the modality standing to prescriptions as 'necessary' stands to descriptive statements.

It seems very natural to say that 'ought' is a deontic modality. This makes rather implausible the argument used by some descriptivists that, since 'His act was wrong' sounds like an ordinary subject–predicate sentence, its surface grammar supports the view that wrongness is a property in the ordinary sense, and thus supports ethical realism. The fact that 'His act was wrong' means much the same as 'He ought not to have done what he did', which has a totally different surface structure, ought to make us at least wonder whether the surface structure of the first sentence is a good guide to its meaning and logic.

If 'ought' (which I shall take as typical of moral words) is a deontic modality governing imperatives, and behaves like the necessity operator, then 'ought'-sentences will entail imperatives, and hence be prescriptive, and hence satisfy my requirement (2), practicality. Since the properties ascribed to moral words by my theory are purely formal, logical properties, it will also satisfy requirement (1), neutrality. Logic is neutral between substantial opinions or claims. This, you will realize, is how my theory escapes that relativism that is the fate of all descriptivist theories. Because the account it gives of moral language is formal, and in particular because it incorporates the formal features of prescriptivity and universalizability, its account can be accepted by different cultures with different moralities. These formal features can be common to all their languages, even though the material features of their moralities, and with them the descriptive meanings of their moral words, and the truth conditions of their moral statements, differ widely.

Since there is a deontic logic, the theory satisfies requirement (4), logicality. And in particular it satisfies requirement (3), incompatibility. Just as two people who say, one of them that some proposition is necessarily true, and the other that it is not necessarily true, are really contradicting each other, so two people who say, one of them that an action is obligatory, and the other that it is not obligatory, are really contradicting each other. I have already begun to show that the theory satisfies requirement (5), arguability, by showing how arguments on Kantian lines, using the universalizability and the prescriptivity of moral statements, can be conducted. I have also already shown that the theory guarantees prescriptivity.

But it guarantees universalizability too. If 'ought' behaves like a necessity operator governing imperatives, it will be the case that 'ought'-statements will be universalizable, just as statements of necessity are. One cannot say that in such-and-such a case something is necessarily so, but that there could be another identical case in which it was not necessarily so. This is true about logical necessity; if one statement is true by logical necessity, then any other sentence of the same logical form will also be necessarily true. It is also true about causal necessity. If one event follows another by causal necessity, then an exactly similar event in identical circumstances must by causal necessity be followed by an exactly similar event. That is precisely analogous to what the thesis of universalizability holds to be true of 'ought'-statements (H 1984*b*). So the two main props of Kantian arguments, universalizability and prescriptivity, are both provided by the theory.

7.6. It is now time to revert to the subject of truth conditions, and to connect them with the feature of universalizability which I have just been discussing. You will remember that earlier I spoke of an element in the meaning of moral statements which I called, following Stevenson, the descriptive meaning. I also said that the objectivistic naturalists had hold of an important truth about this. Though they were wrong in thinking that application conditions for the moral words gave *the meaning* of moral statements, they were right to hold that moral words do have application conditions, and that these do determine truth conditions for moral statements. They were also right, against the intuitionists and the subjectivists, to hold that these application conditions can be given in non-moral, objective terms. They were wrong, however, to think that to say what the application conditions were was a mere matter of definition; it is in fact to state a moral principle of substance.

It should be evident by now that the same animal is here appearing in different metamorphoses. It does not make any difference whether we speak of criteria of application for a moral word (for example 'wrong'), or about the word's descriptive meaning, or about the truth conditions of statements containing it, or about a moral standard or universal moral principle. To endorse any of these is to make a synthetic, substantial, moral statement. The crucial question for ethical theory is how we are to set about deciding rationally *which* criteria, or truth conditions, or standards, or principles, to endorse. As we have also seen, different cultures will have different ones. But we now have a way, a recognizably Kantian way, of adjudicating between them. So our theory no longer leads to relativism. And it was the introduction of prescriptivity and its logic that made this possible.

But why is it appropriate to speak of *truth* in this context? We shall not understand this until we have looked quite deeply into the human circumstances—the social environment—in which we do our moral thinking. All the Kantian approach immediately yields are *maxims* or universal prescriptions. There is no obvious reason yet why we should call these true or false. Could we not, in our moral thinking, make do just with such universal imperatives, and forget about truth and falsehood? The answer is that archangels perhaps could do this, but humans cannot.

I have in my other writings suggested, following Plato, that there are two levels of moral thinking, the critical and the intuitive, of which the second is a necessity for humans (e.g. *MT* 2.1 ff.). The fact that most of our moral thinking is at the intuitive level will help explain why we call moral judgements true or false. To take Harman's example (1977: 4), faced with some boys who have poured petrol over a cat and set it alight, just for fun, we have no hesitation in saying that they have done wrong. Or to take the example I used myself, we do not hesitate to say that it would be wrong to slip away from a petrol station without paying (5.2). We do not feel the need to criticize the standards or principles which make us say these things, or to ask *why* these acts are wrong. So it is easy to say that it is *obviously true* that they are wrong. That is what gives intuitionism its plausibility, and has got it the name of 'the moral philosophy of the man in the street'.

It also gives some plausibility to objectivistic naturalism. Such a naturalist might say, 'If you don't know that those acts are wrong, can you really understand the meaning of "wrong"?' What has happened in such cases is that the descriptive meaning has taken over, almost. It has not taken over completely, because even a person who thinks it 'obviously wrong' to do these things will also normally agree that someone who thinks an act wrong will think that that is a reason for not doing it. So the prescriptivity, though submerged by the descriptive meaning, is still there. But if the moral statement is unquestioned, it is easy to be either an intuitionist or an objectivistic naturalist. If one is not a philosopher, one will not even ask *which* of these one is. I hope you will see how natural it is to say, about such cases, that the moral statements made are true.

7.7. There is a problem which troubled Socrates and Aristotle, and is thought to create difficulties for modern prescriptivists and internalists like me. An internalist, who thinks that to hold a moral opinion is to be motivated to act on it, or to want others to act on it, and a prescriptivist, who thinks that moral statements entail imperatives, are thought to be in difficulties about people who do what they acknowledge to be wrong. There are some people who do what they think wrong because they are in pursuit of other ends that they cannot attain without doing wrong; and there are others whose end *is* to do wrong, just because it is wrong. Let us call the first kind of person the *acratic* and the second the *satanist*. I have dealt at length with these characters in other places (*FR* ch. 5, *MT* 3.7, H 1992*d*: ch. 6, 1992*e*: ii. 1304, 1995*b*, 1996*e*). But I should like to point out here that the existence of these two levels of moral thinking makes the problem much easier to solve. If moral statements have firm descriptive meanings and truth conditions, it is easy to see how someone could have a grasp of the truth of a moral statement but act contrary to the prescription contained in it.

Suppose that the person at the petrol station is sorely tempted to slip away without paying, because he wants to keep his money. He might say that he knows that it would be wrong, or that it is true that it would be wrong. His intuition assures him of this. He has the experience of 'knowing it would be wrong' which intuitionists call 'moral intuition'. How easy it is for somebody in such a situation to ignore the prescriptivity of the statement and so do the act which he 'knows is wrong'! Again, suppose that the boys who burn the cat know that burning the cat satisfies the truth conditions accepted in their culture for the statement that it would be wrong. That may be what makes it attractive for them, if they are malcontents or rebels or alienated from the values of the culture. But in virtue of the descriptive meaning and accepted truth conditions of the statement that it would be wrong, they know it to be true. So, like the man at the petrol station, they ignore the prescriptivity of the statement. But for a detailed treatment of such cases I must refer you to my other writings cited.

I hope I have explained the sense in which moral statements can be true, or even obviously true. But, as I have explained earlier at great length, we cannot stop there. For the 'obvious truth' of such statements is relative to a culture. Our ancestors did not think it obviously true that bear-baiting was wrong. Spaniards now do not think it obviously true that bullfighting is wrong, and *their* ancestors did not think it obviously true that burning *people* was wrong, if they were heretics. The Romans did not think it obviously true that it was wrong to burn people, if they were Christians. So it does make sense to ask *why* moral statements, which we all think are obviously true, *are* true, or even whether they really are true. Unless we are able to ask and answer such questions, our morality will be vulnerable. At times, like the time of Socrates and like our own time, morality can actually be in danger because of the failure to ask and answer them. Socrates thought that the way to answer them was by a new kind of thinking: what I am calling *critical* thinking.

The task of critical thinking is to examine the various standards, or application conditions, or criteria, or truth conditions, or principles, that we find in a given culture, and see whether they can be defended. In critical thinking there can be no appeal to intuitions, nor to descriptive meanings. They are what are being examined. Reliance on them will always land us in relativism. That, in the end, is why we have to reject all forms of descriptivism. The move which enables us to examine them objectively, without being trapped in our own culture, is the Kantian move, the introduction of prescriptivity, and in particular of universal prescriptivity. This *formal* requirement, common to all cultures that ask moral questions, is what constrains us objectively. It is when we ask 'Can I *prescribe*, or *will*, that this maxim should become a universal law?' that we are on firm ground in our moral thinking.

If this discussion could go on longer, I would add something to connect up the formal argument I have been setting out with its practical consequences. These are very great. In my books I have shown how this formal argument yields rules of moral reasoning that will bring us to moral principles which are the same as one kind of utilitarian would come to. I have even been bold enough to call my own theory of moral argument a utilitarian theory, although it does not contain any 'principle of utility', but only a rational *method* for arriving at these particular moral principles (1996c: s.f.).

In Chapter 8 I shall try to show that there is nothing paradoxical in arriving at utilitarian principles via a Kantian method. Though Kant was not a utilitarian, there was nothing in his theory of the Categorical Imperative that prevented him being one, and perhaps he would have been one but for two things. The first was his strict upbringing on highly rigorist principles, which he never shook off. He thought he had to defend these principles (such as the absolute duty to enforce capital punishment, the absolute and exceptionless wrongness of lying—even the sinfulness of masturbation), by appeal to his theory. This had regrettable effects on the way he expounded the theory. But in itself the theory is consistent with the adoption of utilitarian principles.

All this would not have been so bad if it had not been for a second thing that misled him. He seems to have thought that moral principles had to be *simple*. You may remember that in 5.8 I spoke of the confusion that many people still make between universality and generality. This confusion goes back to Aristotle's use of the term '*kath' holou*' for both concepts. I think Kant was a victim of this confusion. It may have led him to insist that moral principles should be highly general (that is, simple), when all they had to be was universal (which is consistent with their being, if need be, quite specific).

I have tried to amend this defect in Kant's exposition of his theory by, in my own writings, distinguishing between two levels of moral thinking, the critical and the intuitive. At the intuitive level our moral thinking has indeed to cleave to general principles (though not, I hope, quite so general as those which inspired Kant's parents when they were bringing him up). But at the critical level at which we assess our intuitive principles, and possibly reject or amend them, our thinking can deal in principles as specific as we need. So the requirement to universalize our maxims does not compel us to adopt very general maxims at this level. All we have to do is to treat similarly all cases having the same *universal* properties, however specific, including cases in which the individuals change roles, and in which therefore we may find ourselves in the position of victim. Such critical thinking may, indeed, lead us to adopt quite general principles for use at the intuitive level; but the thinking which goes to their adoption does not itself *rely* on these general intuitive principles, but only on the requirement to *universalize* our maxims.

7.8. I will end on a very practical note. We started off with a number of down-to-earth moral issues on which I claimed that moral philosophy could shed light. Now it is time to say what light it has shed. The general procedure for settling moral questions should now be clear. It consists in examining in a factual way the consequences of alternative actions and policies, and asking whether we are prepared to prescribe universally their implementation. This is the task of critical thinking. We then need to condense this vast quantity of information into a simpler set of guidelines or intuitive principles for use in our daily life. The task might seem impossible but for one thing: we are not the first to address it. People throughout many generations have faced the problem, and arrived at their solutions. We may expect most of these solutions to be wise ones, because they have been devised by people with a lot of experience of similar problems, and of the consequences of pursuing various solutions to them.

But some of these solutions may have been bad ones. There is nothing infallible about the wisdom of the ages. We can alter our intuitive principles, though with difficulty, if we wish. That is the task of critical thinking. But we should be cautious. Those who have thrown over the accumulated intuitions wholesale have often come to regret it. There is usually more to learn than to discard from the legacy of the past.

The question of whether we should become pacifists, with which I started (2.2), is fairly easily settled (H 1985b). The consequence of not enough people standing up for justice and decency in international relations would be that those who rejected them would have their way, with disastrous consequences for almost everybody. What justice and decency require is a further question, which is to be solved by another application of critical thinking. The answer is provided by a set of guidelines for international politics such that adherence to them does the best, all in all, for those affected. These guidelines are not so hard to find (see e.g. J. E. Hare and C. Joynt 1982).

The questions of abortion and euthanasia, and other questions in medical ethics, have been widely discussed, and I have nothing to add to what I have said about them (e.g. H 1974b, 1975c, d, 1988d). Public opinion seems to be coming round to a utilitarian solution to them, with which I would agree.

The question of what to do about youth crime, to which I proposed in 2.4 a tongue-in-cheek solution, is much more difficult, and has received a lot of media attention recently. The general impression seems to be that, in spite of what some politicians have said, prison does not work with young offenders. Should we then hang them, or at least birch them? Should we adopt sharya law like the Saudi Arabians, or revert to the draconian punishments practised in Singapore? The answer lies in a careful examination of the consequences of such punishments, not merely on the offenders, but on society in general. Flogging of violent criminals, ordered by courts, has been abolished within living memory in many societies, and physical punishment of schoolchildren in state schools has been prohibited only quite recently in Britain. It is still permitted in private schools in the United Kingdom, though the courts may come to ban it, especially the European Court. And there is still a lot of support, both in Britain and in the United States, for the death penalty.

It is hard to believe that all the arguments in favour of such changes in the law are good ones, though some probably are. There are also some good arguments on the other side. The whole question needs going into more carefully, in order to find out, if we can, what the effects on society as a whole would be of various treatments of offenders. So long as we are in the dark about the facts (which we are), we shall not be able to determine the best policies. It is not the province of the moral philosopher to find out the facts, but only to probe bad arguments put forward on the basis of the facts, of which there are plenty. The present situation, in which appeals to morality are made in almost total ignorance of what it is and how to argue rationally about it, is not conducive to the adoption of sound policies.

But the tongue-in-cheek proposal that I made was not that we should hang or flog *offenders*, but something more radical: that we should try to catch them *before* they offended and weed them out. This proposal at least we can reject on the basis of already known facts. To begin with, juries would not convict on such grounds, unless public opinion changed more drastically than it is likely to. We should have to abolish the jury system in favour of some more summary way of administering justice. Even an inquisitorial system, such as is in use on the Continent, is unlikely to allow us to weed out potential offenders before they have offended. We should have to go to something like the system of 'justice' practised by the KGB. And there are obvious and sound utilitarian arguments for not doing that.

Suppose, however, that public opinion, prompted by a crime wave, came to favour the weeding-out policy. Then perhaps juries would go along with it. We cannot pre-judge the issue of whether it would be for the best if they did. We have to look at the consequences of their so doing. It is fairly obvious that they would be disastrous. Our whole system of justice is founded on the premiss that nobody is to be punished, let alone killed, for offences that they have not yet committed. It would take an inconceivable shift in opinion to abandon this principle, and the consequences of its abandonment would be dire. The 'slippery slope' argument, often abused by anti-abortionists, is really cogent here; if there were a danger of our sliding down this slope, we ought to dig in our heels fast. But there is in fact no danger, because we have learnt that safeguards of this sort really are necessary to constrain the adminstration of justice. (For justice and punishment, see further *MT* 9.6 ff., H 1978*d*, 1986*f*.)

I have used this extreme example in order to illustrate how to argue about moral questions. In less extreme examples there can be legitimate differences of opinion which are not so easy to resolve. But the same procedure can be used in resolving them. First we have to work out the consequences of alternative policies, and then find guidelines which will on the whole, if generally adopted, lead to the best courses of action. And the best courses of action are those which do the best, all in all, for people in society, counting each for one and nobody for more than one—i.e. treating each individual as an end. In short, we have to combine the lessons which we ought to have learnt from Kant and Mill.

PART III

KANT

8

COULD KANT HAVE BEEN A UTILITARIAN?

... the supreme end, the happiness of all mankind
(*KrV* A851 = B879 = 549)

The law concerning punishment is a Categorical Imperative; and woe to him who rummages around in the winding paths of a theory of happiness, looking for some advantage to be gained by releasing the criminal from punishment or by reducing the amount of it ...
(*Rl* A196 = B226 = 331)

8.1. My aim in this chapter is to ask a question, not to answer it. To answer it with confidence would require more concentrated study of Kant's text than I have yet had time for. I have read his main ethical works, and formed some tentative conclusions which I shall diffidently state. I have also read some of his English-speaking disciples and would-be disciples, but not, I must admit, any of his German expositors except Leonard Nelson. But my purpose in raising the question is to enlist the help of others in answering it.

To many the answer will seem obvious; for it is an accepted dogma that Kant and the utilitarians stand at opposite poles of moral philosophy. This idea has been the current orthodoxy at least since, in the

Revised from H 1993*a*.

early twentieth century, Prichard and Ross, deontologists themselves, thought they had found a father in Kant. John Rawls, in turn, has been deeply influenced by these intuitionist philosophers, and does not think it necessary to document very fully the Kantian parentage of their views. As a result, the story that Kant and utilitarians have to be at odds is now regularly told to all beginner students of moral philosophy.

But is it true? My own hesitant answer would be that it is not. The position is more complicated. Kant, I shall argue, *could* have been a utilitarian, though he *was* not. His formal theory can certainly be interpreted in a way that allows him—perhaps even requires him—to be one kind of utilitarian. To that extent what J. S. Mill says about the consistency of his own views with Kant's Categorical Imperative is well founded (1861: ch. 5, middle). But Kant's rigorous puritanical upbringing had imbued him with some moral views which no utilitarian—indeed, which few modern thinkers of any persuasion—would be likely to endorse: about capital punishment, for example, and about suicide, and even about lying. These rigoristic views he does his best (unsuccessfully in the view of most expositors) to justify by appeal to his theory.

I shall be looking at some of these arguments. To deontologists who seek to shelter under Kant's wing they give small comfort; for if his *theory* is consistent with one kind of utilitarianism (what kind, I shall be explaining), it does not do them much good if some of his arguments which most people would now reject are anti-utilitarian in tendency. Kant was, indeed, a deontologist, in the sense that he assigned a primary place to duty in his account of moral thinking. But he was not an intuitionist of the stamp of Prichard and Ross. He did not believe, with Prichard, that 'If we do doubt whether there is really an obligation to originate A in a situation B, the remedy lies not in any process of general thinking but in getting face to face with a particular instance of the situation B, and then directly appreciating the obligation to originate A in that situation' (1912: *s.f.*). Kant would have called this 'fumbling about with the aid of examples' (*Tappen vermittelst der Beispiele, Gr* BA36 = 412).

On the contrary, though in the *Groundwork* he respects what he calls 'ordinary rational knowledge of morality', and throughout his writings is happy when common moral convictions support his views, the title of the first chapter shows that he is engaged in a 'transition' from this to 'philosophical knowledge'. The second chapter is called, likewise, 'Transition from Popular Moral Philosophy to Metaphysic of Morals'. Kant would not have been content, as Prichard was and as many of our contemporaries are, and as Rawls almost is, to rely on our ordinary moral convictions as data, even after reflecting on them. Instead, he developed a highly complex and sophisticated account of moral *reasoning*: the 'Metaphysic of Morals'.

In this he was right. Moral philosophy, which Prichard thought rested on a mistake (1912: title), began when Socrates and Plato, faced with a collapse of popular morality because of the inability of its adherents to provide reasons for thinking as they did, set out in the search for these reasons. Kant is in this tradition; Prichard and Ross are not, and Rawls, in some respects their follower, is half in and half out of it. He is only half a rationalist, and half an intuitionist, in that he relies on intuitions altogether too much (H 1973a). This chapter is the beginning of an attempt to rescue Kant from some of his modern 'disciples'.

8.2. I want first to draw attention to some passages in the *Groundwork* which bear on my question. I will start with the famous passage, beloved of anti-utilitarians, about treating humanity as an end. In full it runs: 'Act in such a way that you always treat humanity, whether in your own person or in the person of any other, never simply as a means, but always at the same time as an end' (*Gr* BA66 f. = 429). To understand this we have to know what Kant means by 'treat as an end'. He gives us some important clues to this in the succeeding passage, but unfortunately he seems to be using the expression in at least two different senses. Broadly speaking, the first and third of his examples, those concerned with duties to oneself, are inconsistent with a utilitarian interpretation, but the second and fourth, those concerned with duties to others, are consistent with it. As we shall see, this difference is no accident.

I will take the second and fourth examples first. The second concerns false promises. He combines this with similar examples about 'attempts on the freedom and property of others'. The fault in all such acts lies, he says, in 'intending to make use of another man *merely as means* to an end he does not share (*in sich enthalte*). For the man whom I seek to use for my own purposes by such a promise cannot possibly agree with my way of behaving to him, and so cannot himself share the end of the action'. Other people 'ought always at the same time to be treated as ends—that is, only as beings who must themselves be able to share in the end of the very same action'.

The fourth example I will quote in full:

Fourth, as regards meritorious duties to others, the natural end which all men seek is their own happiness. Now humanity could no doubt subsist if everybody contributed nothing to the happiness of others but at the same time refrained from deliberately impairing their happiness. This is, however, merely to agree negatively and not positively with *humanity as an end in itself* unless every one endeavours also, so far as in him lies, to further the ends of others. For the ends of a subject who is an end in himself must, if this conception is to have its *full* effect in me, be also, as far as possible, *my* ends.

I interpret this as meaning that, in order to fulfil this version of the Categorical Imperative, I have to treat other people's ends (i.e. what they will for its own sake) as *my* ends. They must be able to do the same, i.e. share the end. In the *Tugendlehre* Kant explains the relation between an end and the will as follows: 'An *end* is an object of the power of choice (*Willkür*) (of a rational being), through the thought of which choice is determined to an action to produce this object' (*Tgl* A4 = 381). We shall be examining later the distinction between '*Wille*' and '*Willkür*', and the alleged distinction between will and desire. On this, see esp. *Tgl* A 49 = 407, where *Wille* is *both* distinguished from *Willkür, and* identified with a kind of desire: '*nicht der Willkür, sondern des Willens, der ein mit der Regel, die er annimmt, zugleich allgemein-gesetzgebendes Begehrungsvermögen ist, und eine solche allein kann zur Tugend gezählt werden*' ('not a quality of the power of choice, but of the *will*, which is one with the rule it adopts and which is also the appetitive power as it gives universal law. Only such an aptitude can be called virtue').

Elsewhere Kant qualifies this explanation of what it is to treat others as ends, by saying that the ends of others which we are to treat as our own ends have to be not immoral (*Tgl* A119 = 450: '*die Pflicht, anderer ihre Zwecke (so fern diese nur nicht unsittlich sind) zu den meinen zu machen*)'. Some utilitarians, for example Harsanyi, take a similar line and rule out immoral or anti-social ends from consideration (1988c: 96). I am tempted to say, in the light of the similarity between the views of these utilitarians and Kant, and of the passages we have been discussing, that he *was* a sort of utilitarian, namely a rational-will utilitarian. For a utilitarian too can prescribe that we should do what will conduce to satisfying people's rational preferences or wills-for-ends—ends of which happiness is the sum.

We may notice in passing that this same passage in Kant (*Gr* BA69 = 430) provides an answer to self-styled Kantians who use what has been one of their favourite objections to utilitarianism, that utilitarians do not 'take seriously the distinction between persons' (Rawls 1971: 27; see Mackie and Hare in H 1984g: 106, Richards and Hare in H 1988c : 256). It is hard to understand precisely what the objection is. Clearly utilitarians are as aware as anybody else that different and distinct persons are involved in most situations about which we have to make moral judgements. Probably what the objectors are attacking is the idea that we have, when making a moral decision about a situation, to treat the interests, ends, or preferences of different people affected by our actions as of equal importance, strength for strength. This is the same as to show equal concern and respect for all (another slogan of the objectors, which seems inconsistent with the one we are considering). In other words, I am to treat the interests of the others on a par with my own. This, according to utilitarians, is what is involved in being fair to all those affected. It is to obey Bentham's injunction 'Everybody to count for one, nobody for more than one' (*ap.* Mill 1861: last chapter). And if we treat equal preferences as of equal weight, utilitarianism is the result.

But that is precisely what Kant is telling us to do in this passage, as Mill observes (ibid.). For if I make the ends of others my ends, I shall, in adjudicating between them when they conflict, treat them in the same way as I would my own ends. In so doing I am not failing to distinguish between different people, but, as justice demands, giving equal weight to their and my equal interests (the ends which they and I seek with equal strength of will), just as I give equal weight to my own equal interests. So, if the objection did undermine utilitarianism, it would undermine Kant too.

8.3. But now we have to turn to Kant's first and third examples. In the first, he is against suicide because it involves 'making use of a person merely as a means to maintain a tolerable state of affairs till the end of his life'. But this is not the same sense of 'use as a means' as that which contrasts with 'treat as an end' in the second and fourth examples. I might have as an end the saving myself from intolerable pain. Obviously there is no difficulty in my sharing this end with myself, or agreeing with my way of behaving to myself. Kant must therefore be here using 'use as means' and 'treat as an end' in some different sense. I shall not here investigate what it is; but it seems to be something like 'regard (or not regard) a human being (myself) as at my own disposal to do what I like with for my own purposes'.

But this objection to suicide, if valid at all, is different from those to promise-breaking and non-beneficence. To treat myself as at my own disposal is not to frustrate the ends that I will. Perhaps Kant is here harking back to something he heard when young, that man is created as a human being to fulfil an end ordained by God, and therefore ought not to act contrary to God's will by not fulfilling God's ends. But to argue thus would be to follow a principle of heteronomy such as he later rejects (*Gr* BA92 = 443). It cannot be turned into an autonomous principle by simply substituting 'myself' for 'God'. For if it is not God's will but my will that is in command, then it can, within a consistent set of ends, choose suicide in these special circumstances.

The same could be said about the third example concerning the cultivation of one's talents. For a full statement of the example we have to refer back to *Gr* BA55 = 423. I shall discuss this earlier use of the example shortly. Here it is to be noted that Kant speaks of 'nature's purpose for humanity in our person' (*Gr* BA69 = 430), thus again betraying the theological and heteronomous source of his argument here. A person could certainly with consistency will as *his* end (whatever *nature* intended) to live like the South Sea Islanders of whom Kant has earlier spoken slightingly; and he could certainly share this end with himself, and agree to it. So the sense of 'treat as an end' used in the second and fourth examples would provide no argument at all against his 'devoting his life solely to idleness, indulgence, procreation, and in a word, to enjoyment' (*Gr* BA55 = 423). In the sense used in the second and fourth examples, treating humanity in myself as an end would not preclude my lotus-eating, any more than it would preclude suicide.

I should like to mention here that in my own adaptation of the Kantian form of argument in *FR* ch. 8 I specifically excluded from its scope personal ideals not affecting other people, and said that about these one could not argue in this way. So my view on these first and third examples of Kant is that he is going astray through trying (in order to buttress his inbred convictions) to use arguments from universalizability outside their proper field, which is duties to other people.

There is a possible objection to the assimilation of wills to preferences that I have just made: that a preference, being something empirical, is not the same as a will, which is, in the pure Kantian doctrine, something noumenal (cf. *KpV* A74 f. = 43). To this objection I shall return (8.8).

8.4. But now we must turn to another famous passage, the formulation of the Categorical Imperative which runs: 'Act only on that maxim through which you can at the same time will that it should become a universal law' (*Gr* BA52 = 421).

This version too is consistent with utilitarianism. If we are going to will the maxim of our action to be a universal law, it must be, to use the jargon, universalizable. I have, that is, to will it not only for the present situation, in which I occupy the role that I do, but also for all situations resembling this in their universal properties, including those in which I occupy all the other possible roles. But I cannot will this unless I am willing to undergo what I should suffer in all those roles, and of course also get the good things that I should enjoy in others of the roles. The upshot is that I shall be able to will only such maxims as do the best, all in all, impartially, for all those affected by my action. And this, again, is utilitarianism. To link it up with the other formula about treating people as ends: if I am to universalize my maxim, it must be consistent with seeking the ends of all the other people on equal terms with my own.

This formulation of the Categorical Imperative is followed by another rather similar one: 'Act as if the maxim of your action were to become through your will a universal law of nature' (*Gr* BA 52 = 421). After this, Kant illustrates these two formulations with the same examples as we have been discussing in connection with the 'humanity as an end' formulation. Here again the promise-keeping and beneficence examples fit well with a utilitarian interpretation, but the suicide and cultivation-of-talents examples do not. In the promising case, he uses a form of argument usually now called by English-speaking writers utilitarian generalization; he asks 'How would things stand if my maxim became a universal law?', and answers that promises would become 'empty shams'. This is not a strong argument, because one might will as a universal law that people should break promises in precisely one's own present situation, when one can get away with it and the institution of promising would survive. (Recent work on the difficulty of drawing a line between act- and rule-utilitarianism is relevant here; cf. *FR* 130 ff., Lyons 1965: ch. 3). The argument against promise-breaking we considered earlier, which says that the victim cannot share the end of the promise-breaker, is much stronger, and is similar to one I would myself, as a utilitarian, rely on (H 1964*d*: *s.f.*).

Kant's argument here against non-beneficence comes to much the same as the one I discussed earlier, and one which I should myself, as a utilitarian, employ, and I have no time to analyse it further. The argument against suicide is again very weak. I could certainly without contradiction will universally that those who would otherwise have to endure intolerable pain should kill themselves. This could indeed become a universal law of nature, and I could act as if it were to become so through my will. Kant thinks it is a good argument only because he thinks (perhaps owing to his rigorist upbringing) that maxims have to be very simple. If we have a choice between the simple maxims 'Always preserve human life' and 'Destroy human life whenever you please', we shall probably opt for the former. But there are many less simple maxims in between these extremes which most of us would will in preference to either of them: for example 'Preserve people's lives when that is in their interests' (and perhaps we would wish to add other qualifications). As we have seen (8.1) moral principles do not have to be as simple and general as Kant seems to have thought, and they can still be universal all the same (H 1972a, 1994b).

As regards cultivation of talents, Kant is also on shaky ground. It is perfectly possible to will that those who are in the fortunate position of being able to live like the South Sea Islanders should do so; and this could become a law of nature if nature were as benign everywhere as it is said to be in Tahiti. The best argument against lotus-eating is a utilitarian one, which Kant does not use though he could have; namely that one person's indolence may, in the *actual* state of nature, harm others whom he might be helping if more industrious, and who therefore cannot share his ends.

8.5. The score at this point is that Kant's *theory*, in the formulations of the Categorical Imperative we have considered, is compatible with utilitarianism, and so are some arguments that he uses, or could have used consistently with the theory, in some of his examples. By my reckoning the first example (suicide) is the only one that cannot be handled in a utilitarian way in accordance with the Categorical Imperative in these three formulations, although Kant himself *does* handle both this and the third example in a non-utilitarian way. So, as I said at the beginning, Kant *could* have been a utilitarian, in the sense that his theory is compatible with utilitarianism, but in some of his practical moral judgements his inbred rigorism leads him into bad arguments which his theory will not really support. I do not think that this score ought to give much comfort to modern anti-utilitarians who usurp Kant's authority.

It does, however, emerge from his discussion of the examples in the *Groundwork* that there is a tension in Kant's thought between utilitarian and non-utilitarian elements. How this tension is to be resolved becomes a little clearer in the *Doctrine of Virtue*. There, a main division is made between duties to oneself and duties to others. This distinction and other related ones are laid out in *Tgl* A34 = 397, in the top half of a table headed 'The Material Element of Duty of Virtue'. '*My own end*, which is also my duty' is said to be 'my own *perfection*'; and '*the end of others*, the promotion of which is also my duty' is said to be 'the *happiness* of others'.

The immediate impression we get from this is that there is a utilitarian part of Kant's theory, and a non-utilitarian part. The utilitarian part prescribes duties to others, and these are compatible with utilitarianism (qualified by the requirement, as above, that we have to advance others' ends only in so far as they are consistent with morality). But the other part (duties to oneself) seems to be not utilitarian at all, but perfectionist. However, these impressions are too superficial. This becomes apparent if (taking a hint from what he says against perfectionism in *Gr* BA92 = 443) we ask, first, in what the perfection is supposed to consist; and secondly, what 'consistent with morality' is to mean. As we answer these questions we shall see that the tension between the utilitarian and non-utilitarian elements in Kant's theory begins to ease.

Obviously the perfection that Kant is after is moral perfection. It consists in the acquisition of *virtue*. Part of this virtue will clearly consist in the disposition to fulfil the duties to others laid down on the utilitarian side of the table. But what is the other part? That is, what *content* does moral perfection have, for Kant, over and above the utilitarian content consisting in practical love for other people. (For the notion of 'practical love' see *Gr* BA13 = 399 and *Tgl* A118 f. = 448 f.). It begins to look as if moral perfection, if it sought anything beyond this practical love, would be chasing its own tail. As he says in *Gr* BA92 = 443, '[the ontological concept of perfection] shows an inevitable tendency to go round in a circle and is unable to avoid presupposing the morality it has to explain'. There would be nothing *else* in the duty to make ourselves perfect, except the duty to make ourselves disposed to make ourselves perfect. It would still not have been determined what the perfection, or the performance of the duty to promote it, would consist in.

But we must be careful here to distinguish between form and content. It could be that Kant's view is this: the perfection we are after is one of form, not of content. To explain this: a morally perfect character, or good will, as he sees it, is one *formed* by its own framing of universal laws in accordance with the Categorical Imperative. In seeking moral perfection, we are seeking to make our wills good in this sense. If this is what Kant means, then the utilitarian and the non-utilitarian part of his morality at once come together again. For a will that wills universally must, as we have seen, be a will that treats the ends of other people's wills on equal terms with its own ends; and this is another way of expressing the practical love that we have already found to be required by our duties to others. In other words, the moral perfection of a good will is a perfection of form, and the form is the form of practical love, which is utilitarian, in that it seeks to advance the ends of all impartially. The 'material element', referred to in the title of the table, all comes either directly or indirectly from this source.

The same happens when we ask what it means to say that the ends of others which we seek impartially to advance have to be consistent with morality. Here we have to look in passing at what Kant says later in the *Groundwork* about the Kingdom (or Realm) of Ends. A good will has to be one that can be a lawmaking member of such a realm (*Gr* BA77–9 = 435 f.). This is Kant's way of ensuring that the moralities of all rational beings will be consistent with one another. The lawmakers in the Realm of Ends will legislate unanimously, because each is constrained by the universal form of the legislation.

The effect of this is that the ends of others, which we have a duty to advance impartially, are those only which are moral, i.e. which they would retain if they were legislating universally, or forming universal maxims in accordance with the earlier formulations of the Categorical Imperative. But if these maxims, as they must, express practical love, they too will be consistent with utilitarianism. For utilitarianism is, simply, the morality which seeks the ends of all in so far as all can seek them consistently in accordance with universal maxims. If a utilitarian tried to promote ends which were not consistent with such a morality, he would run up against the obstacle that the ends he was promoting would be such as others could not 'share', as

Kant puts it (see above); and so his entire moral system would come apart. It is part of the requirements for a consistent utilitarian morality that it should be able to be shared by all.

We thus see that even the apparently non-utilitarian part of Kant's doctrine of virtue, and of his entire system, turns into utilitarianism at one remove. It does so because even the apparently non-utilitarian virtue of perfection requires aspirants to it to perfect themselves in practical love.

8.6. The objection might be made that, whereas for Kant human perfection is an end in itself, for the utilitarian it is a mediate end, the ultimate end being the furtherance of the ends of all. This objection is analogous to one which has been made against my own theory, that by dividing moral thinking into two levels I have demoted our ordinary intuitive convictions and prima facie principles into a merely instrumental role. For me, it is said, the real moral thinking takes place at the critical level and is utilitarian; what goes on at the intuitive level is only a *means* to help us fulfil, maximally and on the whole, our utilitarian duties as determined by critical thinking. We are to make ourselves into good people, and fulfil our duties, not for its own sake but because that will *conduce* to the greatest good. It is further alleged (e.g. by Bernard Williams, 1988: 189 ff.) that if we took such an attitude to our common moral convictions, they would soon 'erode'; if they are to retain their force for us, we have to treat them as ultimate.

It has always seemed to me that this objection, whether to my own theory or to Kant as I have interpreted him, will not be sustained by anyone who has experience even of *trying* to live a morally good life. It is perfectly possible at the intuitive level to treat moral duty or virtue as ultimate and give them the 'reverence' that Kant demands, while at the same time to recognize that to establish that those traits of character really do constitute virtue, and that those intuitive moral principles really are the ones we should observe, requires more thought than the mere intuition that this is so. I am sure that Kant would have agreed, although he makes his account of the relation between virtue and duty much more obscure by failing to clarify the distinction between levels of moral thinking (see below). It is in this sense that we should understand passages such as *Tgl* A32 = 396:

'that virtue should be its own end and also, because of the merit it has among men, its own reward', and *Tgl* A33 = 397: 'the worth of virtue itself, as its own end, far exceeds the value of any utility and any empirical ends and advantages that virtue may, after all, bring about.'

8.7. Why is the suggestion that Kant could have been a utilitarian thought so bizarre? It has been held that he could not have been for, in the main, two inadequate reasons. The first is that he often stresses that the *Groundwork of the Metaphysic of Morals*, as he calls his book, cannot appeal to anything contingent and empirical; and desires and preferences are of this sort. But here we have to be very careful to distinguish, as Kant insists on our doing, between the empirical and the rational parts of moral philosophy. He certainly thinks that it has both these parts. He says, about those who fail to distinguish the two roles, 'What (such a procedure) turns out is a disgusting hotch-potch (*Mischmasch*) of second-hand observations and semi-rational principles on which the empty-headed regale themselves, because this is something that can be used in the chit-chat of daily life. Men of insight, on the other hand, feel confused by it and avert their eyes with a dissatisfaction which, however, they are unable to cure' (*Gr* BA31 = 409, cf. BAiv = 388).

The important point to get hold of is that his strictures on bringing in empirical considerations apply *only* to what he is doing in this book: only, that is, to the Metaphysic of Morals, and indeed only to its Groundwork. I think it is legitimate to regard the *Groundwork* as a purely logical enquiry into the nature of moral reasoning, and as such it of course must not contain appeals to empirical facts, any more than any other kind of logic. This is the chief thing, as I said, that distinguishes Kant from some of his modern self-styled disciples.

Let us then look at the Kantian programme, or at this interpretation of it, in more detail. It rests on a metaphysical or logical enquiry into the nature of the moral concepts. This has to be the basis of any system of moral reasoning. We have to do it by considering the nature of the concepts only, not anything empirical. Kant believed in the synthetic a priori, and indeed calls his Categorical Imperative the 'practical synthetic a priori' (*Gr* BA50 = 420). But he explains later that the question how such a synthetic a priori proposition is possible and necessary lies outside the bounds of a metaphysic of morals (*Gr* BA95 = 440). The first two chapters of the *Groundwork* (those we have been concerned with), are 'merely analytic' (*Gr* BA96 = 445); he has been 'developing the concept of morality as generally in vogue'. At any rate he would, I am sure, have rightly excluded from this part of his enquiry any empirical data, whether about what actually goes on in people's minds or about anything else, *including* any antecedently held substantial moral judgements; for the only source of these could be something that goes on in people's minds, that is, intuitions. That we have a certain intuition is an empirical fact, and as such is excluded from this part of the enquiry, for the same reason as desires that we contingently have are excluded. Kant explicitly rejects moral sense theories (*Gr* BA91 f. = 442), and would equally have rejected intuitionism of the sort expressed in the quotation from Prichard that I gave earlier. Ordinary people understand, indeed, the *concepts* of morality, but this is no moral sense apprehending the *substance* of morality.

8.8. The elements of Kant's metaphysic of morals that I find most central are its reliance on the pure will, and its insistence that in moral reasoning we have to will universally. What does 'pure' mean, and what does 'reliance' mean? To understand this we have to consider Kant's doctrine of the autonomy of the will. This, he says, is 'the property the will has of being a law to itself (independently of every property belonging to the objects of volition)' (*Gr* BA87 = 440).

Here it is very easy to go astray in one's interpretation of Kant, and attribute to him a nonsense. One way of taking this doctrine would be to say that to be autonomous the will has to have no regard to what in particular it is willing. So, for example, when I am deciding whether to will to tell an untruth, I have to have no regard to the property of this proposed object of my volition, namely that what I should be saying would be untrue. Or, if I am contemplating killing someone, I am not to pay attention to the property of my action that it would consist in bringing about his death. I cannot believe that this is what Kant meant, because he certainly thought it relevant to the morality of actions that they were lies or murders.

What then did he mean? I think that what he meant was this. Our will is initially free to will whatever we will. We are not *constrained* to will this or that because of what this or that is. The will is constrained only by what Kant calls 'the fitness of its maxims for its own making of universal law' (*Gr* BA88 = 441). This is what is implied in the 'autonomy' formulation of the Categorical Imperative. That is, it is only the universal form of what we are going to will that constrains us, and not any content. The content gets put in by the will itself. The will can accept only such contents or objects of its volition as can be willed universally. This is the same doctrine as I have myself expressed by saying that moral judgements have to be universal prescriptions.

So interpreted, the doctrine of autonomy would exclude as heteronomous many of the principles advocated by some modern so-called Kantians; for they do seek to constrain the will not just formally but substantially by saying that it has to have certain objects. Such intuitionists not only appeal, though they do not call it that, to something empirical, namely the contingent fact that we have certain intuitions or convictions, but seek to constrain the will and bind it to the substantial content of these convictions. This is most un-Kantian.

Returning, then, to the objection we are considering to calling Kant a utilitarian: the objection says that this cannot be so, because utilitarians appeal to desires or preferences, which are something empirical, and therefore excluded by Kant. To this the answer is first, that they are excluded only from the formal part of his enquiry, but have to be admitted into any application to concrete situations of the form of moral reasoning which the enquiry generates; and secondly, that there is nothing to prevent a *utilitarian* from dividing up his enquiry in the same Kantian way, as for clarity he should, and as I do myself. A utilitarian system also has a pure formal part, which (in my view) needs to rely only on the logical properties of the moral concepts. It operates, indeed, with the *concept* of preference (and whether this is a different concept from that of will needs further discussion); but it does not assume that preferences have any particular content. *What* people prefer is an empirical matter; it has to be ascertained once we start to apply our system of reasoning, but in order to set up the system we do not need to assume that people prefer one thing or another; that is, in setting up the system we look merely at the form of people's preferences, not at their content.

It has to be asked whether Kant's wills are any different in this respect. *Gr* BA64 = 427 would suggest that they are not: 'Practical principles are *formal* if they abstract from all subjective ends'; and this is equally true of the 'Principle of Utility' in those utilitarians who have one, especially if it is expressed in terms of the formal notion of preference-satisfaction. It is an empirical fact that a person wills this or that, just as it is an empirical fact that he prefers this or that. But the form of the will or preference can be the same whatever he wills or prefers, provided that for categorical or moral imperatives, as both the utilitarians and Kant can agree, the form is universal.

That, for both Kant and the utilitarians, is the only formal constraint on the will. However, for both there are material constraints, in the concrete situation in which we are doing the willing. Such constraints are, for example, that if I were to say what I am proposing to say, I should be speaking falsely, or that if I were to pull the trigger I should be killing someone. I have to be able to will *this* universally for all similar cases, and this constrains me because of the empirical fact that in that situation the person I should be lying to does not want, or will, to be deceived (as Kant might put it, he and I cannot 'share' the will that he should be), and the person I should be killing does not want, or will, to be killed. Given that this is the will or preference of the other party, I am constrained by this, and by the form of the reasoning, to treat him as an end by making what he wills my end, or in other words to treat his preference as if it were my own. Otherwise I shall not be able to universalize my maxim.

It may be objected that for Kant the distinction between will and mere preference or desire is fundamental. To this there are three replies. The first is that for Kant there *is* an important distinction between the will which is 'nothing but practical reason' (*Gr* BA36 = 412)—i.e. the rational will—and the will that is the source of maxims whether good or bad, rational or irrational. He calls the latter '*Willkür*' (sometimes translated 'choice'). His Latin equivalent for this is *liberum arbitrium*, and it is the possession of this that gives us free will or autonomy. But this distinction is not much relevant to our present problem; for utilitarianism could easily be expressed in terms of rational will.

Secondly, when Kant draws, as he often does, a contrast between rational will and inclination (*Neigung*), it is often, though not always, *selfish* inclination that he has in mind. An example is *Gr* BA8 = 496. We are not to follow our desires in so far as they are desires for *our own* advantage; that would not be to treat others' ends as our own ends. But of course a utilitarian could agree with this insistence that the desires that determine our moral judgement have to be universal and impartial.

Thirdly, Kant, though he makes a clear distinction between will and inclination (*Neigung*), does not in fact always distinguish desire (*Begierde*) in the relevant sense from will, though he does in *Gr* BA124 = 461. In more than one place he identifies them. In the preface and the introduction to the second Critique there are two definitions, one of the faculty of desire (*Begehrungsvermögen*), and the other of will, which are in almost identical terms (*KpV* A17 n. = 9 n., A29 = 15). Later in the same work he speaks of 'the faculty of desire which is therefore called the will, or the pure will in so far as the pure understanding (which in such a case is called reason) is practical through the mere conception of a law' (A96 = 55). From *KU* BAxxiii = 178 n. (different versions in different editions) and *Rl* ABl ff. = 211 ff., it looks as if Kant came to see that there are different things that could be called 'desire', 'inclination', etc. (as indeed there are). If so, it may be that what modern utilitarians call 'preference' might be excluded from his ban on the empirical, and assimilated more to his *Willkür*, or, if rationally universalizing, to his *Wille*.

8.9. Once we have distinguished pure from applied ethics, this first objection to enrolling Kant as a kind of utilitarian collapses. But now we are able to deal with the second objection, that Kant cannot have been a consequentialist, but utilitarians have to be. Once consequentialism is properly formulated, it is hard to see how anyone, Kant included, could fail to be a consequentialist. The doctrine gets a bad name only because its opponents, through their own confusions, formulate it incorrectly (1.8, 7.8, H 1993*c*: 123, 1998*b*).

Let us confine ourselves for the present to moral judgements which are on, or about, acts; for these are the judgements about which consequentialists and anti-consequentialists are supposed to be disagreeing. To act is to make a difference to the course of events, and what the act is, is determined by what difference. To revert to my previous examples (hackneyed ones, I am afraid): if I am wondering whether to pull the trigger, the main morally relevant consideration is that, if I did, the man that my gun is pointing at would die. Killing, which is the morally wrong act, is *causing* death, that is, doing something which has death as a consequence. Similarly, what is wrong about lying is that it is causing someone else to be deceived (to hold a false opinion) by oneself saying something false. The intended consequence is what makes it wrong. It would not be lying if it were not intended to have this consequence.

I am not saying that *all* the consequences of acts are morally relevant. Nor does any utilitarian have to say this. Many will be irrelevant. Which are relevant depends on what moral principles apply to the situation (the relevant consequences are those which the principles forbid or require one to bring about). So what the anti-consequentialists ought to be saying is something that consequentialists who understand the issue can also say: that there are some consequences which are morally relevant, and that we ought to bring about, or not bring about, *those* consequences regardless of the *other* consequences which are morally irrelevant. Thus I ought to speak the truth and so inform the other party of it, even though there will also be the consequence that I am disadvantaged thereby. It is still the intention to bring about the consequence that he is misinformed which makes telling a lie wrong. Kant could not have disagreed.

A further point of objection is related but slightly different. Some of the consequences of actions are intended and some not. When we are speaking of the 'moral worth of the agent', or wondering whether to blame him, it is of course relevant whether he intended the consequences or not. We can say, with Kant, that the only good thing without qualification is a good will (*Gr* BAl = 393), meaning that people are judged by their intentions and not by the actual consequences.

But let us for the present leave aside these *post eventum* judgements and consider the situation of someone who is trying to decide what to do. He is trying to decide what to do intentionally, i.e. what intention to form; for we cannot decide to do something unintentionally (if it were unintentional, we could not speak of our having *decided* to do it). When we are wondering what intention to form, the intentions that are the possible candidates are all intentions to bring about certain consequences; that is, to do certain actions or to make the course of events different in certain ways. So the will itself, which is being formed in this deliberative process, is a will to bring about certain consequences. They are what is willed—the objects of volition, as Kant calls them. So, although the only good thing without qualification is a good will, what makes it a good will is what is willed (autonomously, universally, rationally, and impartially), and that is the consequences that are intended.

Clearly I have been able only to scratch the surface of my question. There are many further points of difficulty in interpreting Kant that I have not had room to raise, let alone discuss. The limit of my ambition has been to get intuitionists, deontologists, and contractualists, who are so sure that Kant was on their side against utilitarianism, to look more carefully at his (admittedly obscure) text. I am confident that, like me, they will at least find many utilitarian *elements* in it.

REFERENCES AND BIBLIOGRAPHY

1. *Complete Bibliography of Writings of R. M. Hare*

References in the text of the form 'H 1971a: 100' are to this part of the bibliography, the last figure being the page except where otherwise indicated. Dates from 1997 are conjectural. References to *The Language of Morals* (1952b), *Freedom and Reason* (1963a), and *Moral Thinking* (1981a) take the form of the letters *'LM'*, *'FR'*, and *'MT'*, respectively, followed by the section number. References of the form '5.3' are to sections of this volume. The author is heavily indebted to Ulla Wessels, whose bibliography appears in H 1995a. Reprints and translations into other languages are included where I have records of them, but these are incomplete. Abstracts are given of the more important recent papers.

1949. 'Imperative Sentences', *Mind* 58. Repr. in 1971c.

1950a. Review of E. W. Hirst, *Morality and God*, *Philosophy* 25.

1950b. Review of H. A. Prichard, *Moral Obligation* and *Knowledge and Perception*, *Oxford Magazine* (15 June).

1950c. 'Theology and Falsification', *University* 1. Repr. in A. G. N. Flew and A. MacIntyre, eds., *New Essays in Philosophical Theology* (London: SCM Press, 1955); in R. E. Santoni, ed., *Religious Language* (Bloomington, Ind.: Indiana University Press, 1968); in 1992d; and in other collections. Italian translation in collection ed. by G. Gava (Liviana, 1972).

1951a. 'Freedom of the Will', *Proceedings of the Aristotelian Society*, supp. vol. 25. Repr. in 1972b.

1951b. Review of G. C. Field, *The Philosophy of Plato*, *Mind* 60.

1951c. Review of S. E. Toulmin, *An Examination of the Place of Reason in Ethics*, *Philosophical Quarterly* 1.

1951d. Review of R. Lepley, ed., *Value: A Cooperative Inquiry*, *Mind* 60.

1952a. Review of H. D. Lewis, *Morals and Revelation*, *Philosophy* 27.

1952b. *The Language of Morals* (Oxford: Oxford University Press). Italian translation, Rome: Ubaldini, 1968; German, Frankfurt a. M.: Suhrkamp, 1972; Japanese, Tokyo: Keiso Shobo, 1981; Portuguese, São Paolo: Martins Fontes, 1996. Extracts in Danish translation, Copenhagen: Gyldendalike, 1976.

1954a. Review of E. W. Hall, *What is Value?*, *Mind* 63.

1954b. Review of *The Ethics of Aristotle*, trans. J. A. K. Thompson, *Oxford Magazine* 62 (25 Feb.).

1954c. Review of J. Wisdom, *Philosophy and Psychoanalysis*, *Philosophy* 29.

1955a. 'Universalisability', *Proceedings of the Aristotelian Society* 55. Repr. in 1972b. German translation in G. Grewendorf and G. Meggle, eds., *Seminar: Sprache und Ethik* (Frankfurt a. M.: Suhrkamp, 1974); Spanish in E. Rabossi and F. Salmerón, eds., *Etica y Análisis* 1 (Mexico City: Mexico University Press, 1976).

1955b.'Ethics and Politics' (two articles and letters), *Listener* (Oct.). Spanish translation in *Revista Universidad de San Carlos* 33. First article repr. in 1972d, in M. Wakin, ed., *War, Morality and the Military Profession* (Boulder, Colo.: Westview, 1979), and in P. Werhane, ed., *Ethical Issues in Business* (Englewood Cliffs, NJ: Prentice-Hall, 1991).

1956a. Review of P. H. Nowell-Smith, *Ethics*, *Philosophy* 31.

1956b. Review of U. Scarpelli, *Filosofia analitica e giurisprudenza*, *Mind* 65.

1957a. 'Geach: Good and Evil', *Analysis* 17. Repr. in P. Foot, ed., *Theories of Ethics* (Oxford: Oxford University Press, 1967) and in 1972b. Spanish translation in E. Rabossi and F. Salmerón, eds., *Etica y Análisis* 1 (Mexico City: Mexico University Press, 1976).

1957b. 'Oxford Moral Philosophy' (letters), *Listener* (21 Feb. and 28 Mar.).

1957c. Review of A. J. Ayer, *The Problem of Knowledge* and B. Russell, *Logic and Knowledge*, *Spectator* (4 Jan.).

1957d. 'Are Discoveries about the Uses of Words Empirical?', *Journal of Philosophy* 34. Full version in 1960a.

1957e. Review of J. O. Urmson, *Philosophical Analysis* and A. J. Ayer *et al.*, *The Revolution in Philosophy*, *Philosophische Rundschau* 5 (in German).

1957f. 'Religion and Morals' in B. G. Mitchell, ed., *Faith and Logic* (London: Allen & Unwin).

1959a. 'Broad's Approach to Moral Philosophy', in P. Schilpp, ed., *The Philosophy of C. D. Broad* (New York: Tudor). Repr. in 1971c and in 1971d.

1960a. 'Philosophical Discoveries' (the full version of 1957d), *Mind* 69. Repr. in A. Sesonske and N. Fleming, eds., *Plato's Meno* (Belmont, Calif.: Wadsworth, 1965); R. Rorty, ed., *The Linguistic Turn* (Chicago, Ill.: Chicago University Press, 1967); C. Lyas, ed., *Philosophy and Linguistics* (London: Macmillan, 1971); N. Bowie, ed., *The Tradition of Philosophy* (Belmont, Calif: Wadsworth, 1986); and in 1971c. German translation in G. Grewendorf and G. Meggle, eds., *Linguistik und Philosophie* (Frankfurt a. M.: Athenäum, 1974).

1960*b*. 'A School for Philosophers', *Ratio* 2 (also in German edition). Repr. in 1971*d*.

1960*c*. Review of F. E. Sparshott, *An Enquiry into Goodness*, *Philosophical Quarterly* 10.

1960*d*. '"Rien n'a d'importance": l'anéantissement des valeurs est-il pensable?', also discussion of other papers, in L. Beck, ed., *La Philosophie analytique* (Paris: Minuit). English version, 'Nothing Matters', in 1972*d*. Repr. in T. Beauchamp, ed., *Death and Dying* (Englewood Cliffs, NJ: Prentice-Hall, 1978); E. Klemke, ed., *The Meaning of Life* (New York: Oxford University Press, 1981); J. Halberstam, ed., *Virtues and Values* (Englewood Cliffs, NJ: Prentice-Hall, 1987), and other collections. German translation (abridged) in C. Fehige and G. Meggle, eds., *Der Sinn des Lebens* (Munich: 1995).

1960*e*. 'Ethics', in J. O. Urmson, ed., *Encyclopedia of Western Philosophy and Philosophers* (London: Rainbird). Repr. in M. Lipman, ed., *Growing Up with Philosophy* (Philadelphia, Pa.: Temple University Press, 1978), and in 1972*b*.

1962. Review of M. Singer, *Generalization in Ethics*, *Philosophical Quarterly* 12.

1963*a*. *Freedom and Reason* (Oxford: Oxford University Press). Italian translation, Milan: Il Saggiatore, 1971; German, Düsseldorf: Patmos, 1975, republished Frankfurt a. M.: Suhrkamp, 1983.

1963*b*. 'Descriptivism', *Proceedings of the British Academy* 49. Repr. in W. D. Hudson, ed., *The Is–Ought Question* (London: Macmillan, 1969) and in 1972*b*. German translation in G. Grewendorf and G. Meggle, eds., *Seminar: Sprache und Ethik* (Frankfurt a. M.: Suhrkamp, 1974); Spanish in E. Rabossi and F. Salmerón, eds., *Etica y Análisis* 1 (Mexico City: Mexico University Press, 1976); Serbo-Croat in collection ed. by J. Babi-Avdispabic (Sarajevo: Svjetlost, 1987).

1963*c*. Letter in *Times Literary Supplement* (26 Apr.) on review of *Freedom and Reason*.

1964*a*. 'Pain and Evil', *Proceedings of the Aristotelian Society*, supp. vol. 38. Repr. in J. Feinberg, ed., *Moral Concepts* (Oxford: Oxford University Press, 1969) and in 1972*b*.

1964*b*. 'Adolescents into Adults', in T. C. B. Hollins, ed., *Aims in Education* (Manchester: Manchester University Press). Repr. in 1972*d* and 1992*d*.

1964*c*. 'A Question about Plato's Theory of Ideas', in M. Bunge, ed., *The Critical Approach: Essays in Honor of Karl Popper* (Glencoe, Ill.: Free Press of Glencoe). Repr. in 1971*d*.

1964*d*. 'The Promising Game', *Revue Internationale de Philosophie* 70. Repr. in P. Foot , ed., *Theories of Ethics* (Oxford: Oxford University Press, 1967);

W. D. Hudson, ed., *The Is–Ought Question* (London: Macmillan, 1969); and in 1989*b*. Spanish translation in E. Rabossi and F. Salmerón, eds., *Etica y Análisis* 1 (Mexico City: Mexico University Press, 1976), Polish in *Etyka* (1979).

1964*e*. 'Wat is Leven?', *Elseviers Weekblad* (in Dutch). English version in 1965*b*.

1964*f*. 'The Objectivity of Values', *Common Factor* 1.

1965*a*. Review of G. H. von Wright, *Norm and Action*, *Philosophical Quarterly* 15.

1965*b*. 'What is Life?', *Crucible* (English version of 1964*e*). Repr. in 1972*d*.

1965*c*. 'Plato and the Mathematicians', in R. Bambrough, ed., *New Essays on Plato and Aristotle* (London: Routledge). Repr. in 1971*d*.

1966. 'Peace', RSA Lecture, Australian National University, Canberra, privately printed. Repr. in J. Rachels, ed., *Moral Problems* (New York: Harper & Row, 1970), and in 1972*d*.

1967*a*. 'The Lawful Government', in P. Laslett and W. G. Runciman, eds., *Philosophy, Politics and Society* (Oxford: Blackwell). Repr. in J. Rachels and F. Tillman, eds., *Moral and Social Problems* (New York: Harper & Row, 1971), and 1972*d*.

1967*b*. 'Conventional Morality', 'Decision', 'Deliberation', 'Ethics', 'Intention', and 'Right and Wrong', in J. Macquarrie, ed., *Dictionary of Christian Ethics* (London: SCM Press).

1967*c*. Review of S. Hampshire, *Freedom of the Individual*, *Philosophical Review* 76.

1967*d*. 'Some Alleged Differences between Imperatives and Indicatives', *Mind* 76. Repr. in 1971*c*.

1968*a*. Review of G. J. Warnock, *Contemporary Moral Philosophy*, *Mind* 77.

1968*b*. Review of R. S. Peters, *The Concept of Education*, *Mind* 77.

1969*a*. 'Practical Inferences', in V. Kruse, ed., *Festskrift til Alf Ross* (Copenhagen: Juristforbundets Vorlag). Repr. in 1971*c*.

1969*b*. Review of A. Ross, *Directives and Norms*, *Mind* 78.

1969*c*. 'Community and Communication', in S. Verney, ed., *People and Cities* (London: Fontana). Repr. in 1972*d*.

1969*d*. Review of B. G. Mitchell, *Law, Morality and Religion*, *Philosophy* 44.

1970*a*. 'Meaning and Speech Acts', *Philosophical Review* 79. Repr. in 1971*c*.

1970*b*. 'Condizioni intellettuali per la sopravvivenza dell' uomo', *Proteus* 1.

1970*c*. Reply to R. S. Katz, 'Liberals, Fanatics and Not-so-innocent Bystanders', *Jowett Papers, 1968–1969*, ed. B. Y. Khanbhai *et al.* (Oxford: Blackwell).

1970*d*. General Introduction and Introduction to *Meno* in paperback edition of *The Dialogues of Plato*, trans. B. Jowett, ed. R. M. Hare and D. A. F. M. Russell (London: Sphere Books).

1971*a*. Review of L. van der Post, *The Prisoner and the Bomb*, *New York Review of Books* 17 (20 May).

1971*b*. 'Wanting: Some Pitfalls', in R. Binkley *et al.*, eds., *Agent, Action and Reason* (Toronto, Ont.: Toronto University Press). Repr. in 1971*c*. German translation in A. Beckermann and G. Meggle, eds., *Analytische Handlungstheorie* (Frankfurt a. M.: Suhrkamp, 1985).

1971*c*. *Practical Inferences*, containing 1949, 1969*a*, 1970*a*, 1971*b*, 'Austin's Distinction between Locutionary and Illocutionary Acts', and new appendices (London: Macmillan).

1971*d*. *Essays on Philosophical Method*, containing 1959*a*, 1960*a*, 1960*b*, 1964*c*, 1965*c*, 'The Practical Relevance of Philosophy', and 'The Argument from Received Opinion' (London: Macmillan). Italian translation, Armando, 1977.

1971*e*. 'Drugs and the Role of the Doctor', and other contributions to I. T. Ramsey and R. Porter, eds., *Personality and Science* (Edinburgh: Churchill Livingstone).

1972*a*. 'Principles', *Proceedings of the Aristotelian Society* 73. Repr. in 1989*b*.

1972*b*. *Essays on the Moral Concepts*, containing 1951*a* (part), 1955*a*, 1957*a*, 1960*e*, 1963*b*, 1964*a*, and 'Wrongness and Harm' (London: Macmillan).

1972*c*. 'Rules of War and Moral Reasoning', *Philosophy and Public Affairs* 1. Repr. in M. Cohen *et al.*, eds., *War and Moral Responsibility* (Princeton, NJ: Princeton University Press, 1974), and in 1989*c*.

1972*d*. *Applications of Moral Philosophy*, containing 1955*b* (first article), 1960*d* (English version), 1964*b*, 1965*b*, 1966, 1967*a*, 1969*c*, 'Reasons of State', and 'Function and Tradition in Architecture' (London: Macmillan). Japanese translation, Tokyo: Keiso Shobo, 1981.

1972*e*. Review of G. J. Warnock, *The Object of Morality*, *Ratio* 14 (also in German edition).

1972*f*. 'Wissenschaft und praktische Philosophie', in A Diemer, ed., *Proc. of 9. Deutscher Kongress für Philosophie und Wissenschaft* (Meisenheim: Hain).

1973*a*. Critical Study, 'Rawls' Theory of Justice' I and II, *Philosophical Quarterly* 23. Repr. in N. Daniels, ed., *Reading Rawls* (Oxford: Oxford University Press, 1975), and in 1989*b*.

1973*b*. 'The Simple Believer', in G. Outka and J. P. Reeder, eds., *Religion and Morality* (New York: Anchor Press). Repr. in T. Beauchamp *et al.*, eds., *Philosophy and the Human Condition* (Englewood Cliffs, NJ: Prentice-Hall, 1980), and in 1992*d*.

1973*c*.'Language and Moral Education', in G. Langford and D. J. O'Connor, eds., *New Essays in the Philosophy of Education* (London: Routledge). Repr.

in 1979*d* with criticism by G. J. Warnock and reply, and in 1992*d* with reply only.

1973*d*. 'Sad Moralny (Moral Judgment)', *Etyka* 11 (Warsaw), with abstracts in English and Russian.

1974*a*. Comment on R. Edgley, 'Reason and Violence', in S. Körner, ed., *Practical Reason* (Oxford: Blackwell).

1974*b*. 'The Abnormal Child: Moral Dilemmas of Doctors and Parents', *Documentation in Medical Ethics* 3. Repr. as 'Survival of the Weakest' in S. Gorovitz, ed., *Moral Problems in Medicine* (Englewood Cliffs, NJ: Prentice-Hall, 1976), and in 1993*c*. German translation in A. Leist, ed., *Um Leben und Tod* (Frankfurt a. M.: Suhrkamp, 1990).

1974*c*. 'Platonism in Moral Education: Two Varieties', *Monist* 58. Repr. in 1992*d*. French translation in M. Canto-Sperber, ed., volume of essays on Plato's *Meno* (Paris: Jacob, 1990).

1974*d*. 'What Use is Moral Philosophy', TV discussion with A. J. P. Kenny, in *Philosophy in the Open* (Milton Keynes: Open University).

1975*a*. 'Contrasting Methods of Environmental Planning', in R. S. Peters, ed., *Nature and Conduct*, Royal Institute of Philosophy Lectures (London: Macmillan). Repr. in K. Goodpaster and K. Sayre, eds., *Ethics and Problems of the 21st Century* (Notre Dame: University of Notre Dame Press, 1979), and in 1989*c*.

1975*b*. 'Autonomy as an Educational Ideal', in S. C. Brown, ed., *Philosophers Discuss Education* (London: Macmillan). Repr. in 1992*d*.

1975*c*. 'Abortion and the Golden Rule', *Philosophy and Public Affairs* 4. Repr. in R. Baker and F. Elliston, eds., *Philosophy and Sex* (Buffalo, NY: Prometheus, 1975); in *Moral Problems*, ed. J. Rachels (New York: Harper & Row, 1978); in D. Goldberg, ed., *Ethical Theory and Society* (New York: Holt Rinehart, 1987); and in 1993*c*. German translation in A. Leist, ed., *Um Leben und Tod* (Frankfurt a. M.: Suhrkamp, 1990); Italian in G. Ferranti and S. Maffettone, eds., *Introduzione alla bioetica* (Naples: Liguori, 1991).

1975*d*. 'Euthanasia: A Christian View', *Philosophic Exchange* 2 (Proceedings of Center for Philosophic Exchange). Repr. in 1992*d*.

1976*a*. 'Ethical Theory and Utilitarianism', in H. D. Lewis, ed., *Contemporary British Philosophy* 4 (London: Allen & Unwin). Repr. in A. K. Sen and B. A. Williams, eds., *Utilitarianism and Beyond* (Cambridge: Cambridge University Press, 1982); in D. Barnett, ed., *Western Moral Philosophy* (Mountain View, Calif.: Mayfield, 1994); and in 1989*b*.

1976*b*. 'Some Confusions about Subjectivity', in J. Bricke, ed., *Freedom and Morality* (Lawrence, Kan.: University of Kansas Press). Repr. in 1989*b*.

1976c. 'Political Obligation', in T. Honderich, ed., *Social Ends and Political Means* (London: Routledge). Repr. in 1989c.

1976d. 'Value Education in a Pluralist Society: A Philosophical Glance at the Humanities Curriculum Project', in R. S. Peters, ed., *Proceedings of the Philosophy of Education Society of Great Britain* 10. Repr. in M. Lipman, ed., *Growing Up with Philosophy* (Philadelphia, Pa.: Temple University Press, 1978), and in 1992d.

1976e. Review of H.-N. Castañeda, *The Structure of Morality*, *Journal of Philosophy* 73.

1977a. 'Medical Ethics: Can the Moral Philosopher Help?', in S. Spicker and T. Engelhardt, eds., *Philosophy and Medicine 3: Philosophical Medical Ethics, its Nature and Significance* (Dordrecht: Reidel). Repr. in 1993c.

1977b. 'Geach on Murder and Sodomy' (about 'is'–'ought' derivations), *Philosophy* 52.

1977c. 'Opportunity for What? Some Remarks on Current Disputes on Equality in Education', *Oxford Review of Education* 3. Repr. in 1992d.

1977d. 'Sprawiedliwość i równość', *Etyka* 15 (Warsaw) (in Polish, with abstracts in English and Russian). English version in 1978d, repr. in 1989c. Discussed in 1979h.

1978a. 'Prediction and Moral Appraisal', *Midwest Studies in Philosophy* 3. Repr. in 1993c.

1978b. 'Relevance', in A. Goldman and J. Kim, eds., *Values and Morals* (Dordrecht: Reidel). Repr. in 1989b.

1978c. 'Moral Philosophy', TV interview with B. Magee in his *Men of Ideas* (London: BBC).

1978d. 'Justice and Equality', in J. Arthur and W. Shaw. eds., *Justice and Economic Distribution* (Englewood Cliffs, NJ: Prentice-Hall). Revised English version of 1977d. Repr. in J. Sterba, ed., *Justice: Alternative Political Perspectives* (Belmont, Calif.: Wadsworth, 1991); in W. Kymlicka, ed., *Justice in Political Philosophy* (Aldershot: Elgar, 1992); in L. Pojman and R. Westmoreland, eds., *Equality* (New York: Oxford University Press, 1997); in M. Hajdin, ed., *The Notion of Equality* (forthcoming); and in 1989c. Discussed in 1979h.

1979a. 'What Makes Choices Rational?', *Review of Metaphysics* 32. Repr. in 1989b.

1979b. 'What is Wrong with Slavery', *Philosophy and Public Affairs* 8. Repr. in J. Arthur, ed., *Morality and Moral Controversies* (Englewood Cliffs, NJ: Prentice-Hall, 1979); in P. Singer, ed., *Readings in Applied Ethics*, (Oxford: Oxford University Press, 1986); in T. Lott, ed., *Slavery and Social Philosophy*

(Totowa, NJ: Rowman & Littlefield, forthcoming); and in 1989c. German translation in *Conceptus* 15 (1981).

1979c. 'Non-descriptivist Ethics' and 'Utilitarianism' in W. Reich, ed., *Encyclopedia of Bioethics* (New York: Free Press).

1979d. Reprint of 1973c with criticism by G. J. Warnock and reply, in D. B. Cochrane *et al.*, *The Domain of Moral Education* (Toronto, Ont.: Paulist Press). Repr. without Warnock's criticism in 1992d.

1979e. 'Universal and Past-Tense Prescriptions: A Reply to Mr. Ibberson', *Analysis* 39.

1979f. 'On Terrorism', *Journal of Value Inquiry* 13. Repr. in 1989c.

1979g. 'Utilitarianism and the Vicarious Affects', in E. Sosa, ed., *The Philosophy of Nicholas Rescher* (Dordrecht: Reidel). Repr. in 1989b.

1979h. 'Justice and Equality: Some Comments on the 1979 Symposium in Warsaw', *Dialectics and Humanism* 6 (Warsaw). Contains discussion of 1978d.

1979i. 'Behaviour Therapy and Moral Responsibility', *Midwife, Health Visitor and Community Nurse* (London).

1980a. 'Moral Conflicts', in S. McMurrin, ed., *The Tanner Lectures on Human Values* vol. i (Salt Lake City, Utah: University of Utah Press and Cambridge: Cambridge University Press). Revised in 1981a, chs. 2 f.

1980b. Review of T. Nagel, *Mortal Questions*, *Philosophical Books* 21.

1981a. *Moral Thinking: Its Levels, Method and Point*, with bibliography of R. M. Hare's writings 1971–80 (Oxford: Oxford University Press). Italian translation, Bologna: Il Mulino, 1989; Chinese, Hong Kong: Philosophia, 1992; German, Frankfurt a. M.: Suhrkamp, 1992; Japanese, Tokyo: Keiso, 1994; Swedish, Stockholm: Thales, 1995.

1981b. Review of P. Singer, *The Expanding Circle*, *New Republic* (7 Feb.).

1981c. 'On a Misunderstanding of Geach's', *Analysis* 41.

1981d. 'On the Possibility of a Rational Foundation of Norms', in A. S. Skiadas, ed., *Scientific and Extra-scientific Rationality* (Proceedings of conference of Ellenike Anthropistike Etaireia at Portaria, Thessaly, 1978) (Athens).

1982a. *Plato* (Oxford: Oxford University Press). German translation, Stuttgart: Reclam, 1990; Spanish, Madrid: Alianza, 1992; Malaysian, Kuala Lumpur: DBP, 1993; Romanian, Bucharest: Humanitas, 1997; Polish, Warsaw: Urbanski, forthcoming; Portuguese, Lisbon: Presenca, forthcoming; Indonesian, Jakarta: Grafiti, forthcoming. Repr. in R. M. Hare, J. Barnes, and H. Chadwick, *Founders of Thought* (Oxford: Oxford University Press, 1991), Czech translation, Prague: Svoboda, 1994; Chinese translation forthcoming

1982*b*. 'Utilitarianism and Double Standards: A Reply to Dr. Annas', *Oxford Review of Education* 8.

1982*c*. 'Moral Philosophy: Some Waymarks' (in Hebrew), in A. Kasher and S. Lappin, eds., *New Trends in Philosophy* (Tel Aviv: Yachdav).

1982*d*. Interview with Carl Rudbeck, *Svenska Dagbladet*, Feb. (in Swedish).

1983*a*. 'Philosophical Introduction', in S. Bloch and P. Chodoff, eds., *Psychiatric Ethics* (Oxford: Oxford University Press). Repr. as 'The Philosophical Basis of Psychiatric Ethics', in 1993*c*.

1983*b*. 'On the Scientific Justification of Norms', in A. Diemer, ed., *16. Weltkongress für Philosophie* (Frankfurt a. M.: Peter Lang).

1984*a*. 'Do Agents Have to be Moralists?', in E. Regis, Jr., *Gewirth's Ethical Rationalism* (Chicago, Ill.: University of Chicago Press).

1984*b*. 'Supervenience', *Proceedings of the Aristotelian Society*, supp. vol. 56. Repr. in 1989*b*.

1984*c*. 'Utility and Rights: Comment on David Lyons' Paper', *Nomos* 24: *Ethics, Economics and the Law*. Repr. in 1989*c*.

1984*d*. 'Arguing about Rights', *Emory Law Journal* 33. Repr. in 1989*c*.

1984*e* 'Liberty and Equality: How Politics Masquerades as Philosophy', *Social Philosophy and Policy* 2. Repr. in 1989*c*.

1984*f*. 'Some Reasoning about Preferences: A Response to Essays by Persson, Feldman and Schueler', *Ethics* 95. Repr. in 1989*b*.

1984*g*. 'Rights, Utility and Universalization: a Reply to John Mackie', in R. Frey, ed., *Utility and Rights* (Minneapolis, Minn.: University of Minnesota Press). Repr. in 1989*c*.

1985*a*. 'Ontology in Ethics', in T. Honderich, ed., *Morality and Objectivity: Tribute to J. L. Mackie* (London: Routledge). Repr. in 1989*b*.

1985*b*. 'Philosophy and Practice: Some Issues about War and Peace', in A. P. Griffiths, ed., *Philosophy and Practice* (Royal Institute of Philosophy Lectures 19, supp. to *Philosophy* 59) (Cambridge: Cambridge University Press). Repr. in 1989*c*.

1985*c*. 'Little Human Guinea-Pigs?', in M. Lockwood, ed., *Moral Dilemmas in Modern Medicine* (Oxford: Oxford University Press). Repr. in 1993*c*.

1985*d*. 'The Ethics of Experimentation on Human Children', in R. B. Marcus *et al.*, eds., *Logic, Methodology and Philosophy of Science* 7 (Proceedings of 7th International Congress of Logic, Methodology and Philosophy of Science, Salzburg 1983) (Amsterdam: North Holland). No overlap with 1985*c*.

1985*e*. 'Come decidere razionalmente le questioni morali', in L. Gianformaggio and E. Lecaldano, eds., *Etica e diritto: le vie della giustificazione razionale* (Rome: Laterza). English version in 1986*i*, repr. in 1989*b*.

1985*f*. Comment on T. Beauchamp, 'Manipulative Advertising', *Business and Professional Ethics Journal* 3.

1986*a*. 'A Kantian Utilitarian Approach', in G. Ezorsky, ed., *Moral Rights in the Workplace* (New York: State University of New York Press). Excerpt from 1989*c*, ch. 11.

1986*b*. 'Why Do Applied Ethics?', in R. M. Fox and J. P de Marco, eds., *New Directions in Ethics* (London: Routledge). Repr. in R. Shehadi and D. M. Rosenthal, eds., *Applied Ethics and Ethical Theory* (Salt Lake City, Utah: University of Utah Press, 1988), and in 1989*b*. Italian translation in M. Mori, ed., *Questioni di bioetica* (Rome: Riuniti, 1988).

1986*c*. 'A *Reductio ad Absurdum* of Descriptivism', in S. Shanker, ed., *Philosophy in Britain Today* (London: Croom Helm). Repr. in 1989*b*.

1986*d*. 'Health', *Journal of Medical Ethics* 12. Repr. in 1993*c*.

1986*e*. 'Liberty, Equality and Fraternity in South Africa?', in *South African Journal of Philosophy* 5. Also in *Philosophical Forum* 8 (1986). Repr. in P. Collins, ed., *Thinking about South Africa* (Hemel Hempstead: Harvester Wheatsheaf, 1990), and in 1989*c*.

1986*f*. 'Punishment and Retributive Justice', *Philosophical Topics* 2, *Papers on Ethics*, ed. J. Adler and R. N. Lee. Repr. in 1989*c*.

1986*g*. 'Universalizability' and 'Utilitarianism', and articles listed under 1967*b*, in J. Childress and J. Macquarrie, eds., *New Dictionary of Christian Ethics* (London: SCM Press), also published as *Westminster Dictionary of Christian Ethics* (Philadelphia, Pa.: Westminster Press).

1986*h*. 'Warunkowe i bezwarunkowe obowiazywanie norm moralnych' ('The Conditional and Unconditional Validity of Moral Norms') (reply to Ija Lazari-Pavlowska's paper of the same name), *Etyka* 22 (Warsaw).

1986*i*. 'How to Decide Moral Questions Rationally', *Crítica* 18 (English version of 1985*e*). Repr. in 1989*b*.

1986*j*. Comment on Putnam, *Crítica* 18, Appendix.

1987*a*. 'An Ambiguity in Warnock', *Bioethics* 1.

1987*b*. 'Moral Reasoning about the Environment', *Journal of Applied Philosophy* 4. Repr. in 1989*c*.

1987*c*. Review of B. Mayo, *The Philosophy of Right and Wrong*, *Philosophical Quarterly* 37.

1987*d*. '*In Vitro* Fertilization and the Warnock Report', in R. F. Chadwick, ed., *Ethics, Reproduction and Genetic Control* (London: Croom Helm). Repr. in 1993*c*.

1987*e*. 'Why Moral Language?', in P. Pettit *et al.*, eds., *Metaphysics and Morality: Essays in Honour of J. J. C. Smart* (Oxford: Blackwell). Repr. in 1992*d*.

1987*f*. Comment on J. Kaufman, 'Hamlethics in Planning', *Business and Professional Ethics Journal* 6.

1987*g*. 'Embryo Experimentation: Public Policy in a Pluralist Society', *Bioethics News* 7. Repr. in K. Dawson and J. Hudson, eds., *IVF: The Current Debate* (conference proceedings) (Clayton, Vic.:1987); in H. Kuhse *et al.*, eds., *Embryo Experimentation* (Cambridge: Cambridge University Press, 1990); in K. W. M. Fulford , ed., *Medicine and Moral Reasoning* (Cambridge: Cambridge University Press 1994); and 1993*c*. German translation in H.-M. Sass, ed., *Medizin und Ethik* (Stuttgart: Reclam, 1989).

1987*h*. 'La enseñanza de la ética médica: la contribucion de la filosofia', *JANO* 33.

1988*a*. 'When Does Potentiality Count? A Comment on Lockwood', *Bioethics* 2. Repr. in 1993*c* and in N. Fotion and J. C. Heller, eds., *Contingent Future Persons* (Dordrecht: Kluwer, forthcoming).

1988*b*. 'Possible People', *Bioethics* 2. Repr. in 1993*c*.

1988*c*. Comments on R. B. Brandt, W. K. Frankena, A. Gibbard, J. Griffin, J. C. Harsanyi, W. D. Hudson, T. Nagel, D. A. J. Richards, T. M. Scanlon, P. Singer, J. O. Urmson, Z. Vendler, and B. Williams, in D. Seanor and N. Fotion, eds., *Hare and Critics* (Oxford: Oxford University Press).

1988*d*. 'A Kantian Approach to Abortion' in M. Bayles and K. Henley, eds., *Right Conduct: Theories and Applications* (New York: Random House). Repr. in S. Luper-Foy and C. Brown, eds., *The Moral Life* (New York: Holt Rinehart, 1991), and in1993*c*, and with commentary and reply by R. B. Brandt in *Social Theory and Practice* 15 (1989). Spanish translation in *Dianoia* 36 (1990).

1988*e*. 'The Poverty of Ideas', *Guardian* (11 Oct.). Repr. in *Political Studies Association* (June 1990).

1989*a*. 'Some Sub-atomic Particles of Logic', *Mind* 98.

> Four constituents in the expression of speech acts are distinguished: (1) the sign of mood (indicative, imperative, etc.) or tropic; (2) the sign of subscription or neustic (Frege's judgement-stroke); (3) the sign of completeness or clistic; (4) the indication of the content of the speech act, or phrastic. All contribute to the meaning and logical properties of speech acts. Various ordinary-language signs performing these functions are noticed, and (2) defended against the usual objections of Wittgenstein and others. It is asked which of these particles include which in their scopes, and in what senses truth-value attaches to phrastics with or without the other particles.

1989*b*. *Essays in Ethical Theory* (Oxford: Oxford University Press). Contains 1964*d*, 1972*a*, 1973*a*, 1976*a*, 1976*b*, 1978*b*, 1979*a*, 1979*g*, 1984*b*, 1984*f*, 1985*a*, 1986*b*, 1986*i*, and 1994*d*. Italian translation, Milan: Il Saggiatore, 1992.

1989*c*. *Essays on Political Morality* (Oxford: Oxford University Press). Contains 1972*c*, 1975*a*, 1976*c*, 1978*d*, 1979*b*, 1979*f*, 1984*c*, 1984*d*, 1984*e*, 1984*g*,

1985*b*, 1986*e*, 1986*f*, 1987*b*, 'The Role of Philosophers in the Legislative Process', 'Rebellion', and 'The Rights of Employees: The European Court of Human Rights and the Case of Young, James and Webster'. Italian translation, Milan: Il Saggiatore, 1995; Arabic (in part), Beirut: Saqi, 1996.

1989*d*. 'Brandt on Fairness to Happiness', with reply by R. B. Brandt, *Social Theory and Practice* 15.

1989*e*. 'Una aproximación kantiana a la política sanitaria', *Agora* 8. Repr. in part as 'Health Care Policy: Some Options' in 1993*c*.

1989*f*. Replies to Persson, Rabinowicz, Sandoe, and Wetterström, *Theoria* 55.

1989*g*. Interview with P. Apsden, *Times Higher Education Supplement* (June).

1991*a*. 'Universal Prescriptivism', in P. Singer, ed., *A Companion to Ethics* (Oxford: Blackwell). German translation in C. Fehige and G. Meggle, eds., *Zum moralischen Denken* (Frankfurt a. M.: Suhrkamp, 1995).

1991*b*. 'Are there Moral Authorities?' in D. R. Bromham *et al.*, eds., *Reproductive Medicine* (Berlin: Springer). Repr. in 1992*d*.

1991*c*. 'Kant utilitarista?', *Materiali per una storia della cultura giuridica* 21. English version in 1993*a*, German in C. Fehige and G. Meggle, eds., *Zum moralischen Denken* (Frankfurt a. M.: Suhrkamp, 1995).

1992*a*. 'Morality, Moral Theory and Applied and Professonal Ethics: Reply to Bernard Gert', *Professional Ethics* 1.

1992*b*. 'One Philosopher's Approach to Business and Professional Ethics', *Business and Professional Ethics Journal* 11. Repr. in C. Cowton and R. Crisp, eds., *Business Ethics* (Oxford: Oxford University Press, forthcoming).

1992*c*. 'What are Cities For? The Ethics of Urban Planning', in C. C. W. Taylor, eds., *Ethics and the Environment* (Oxford: Corpus Christi College). German translation in 1995*a*; Italian in S. Moroni, ed., collection on planning and social justice (Milan: Franco Angeli, forthcoming).

1992*d*. *Essays on Religion and Education* (Oxford: Oxford University Press). Contains 1950*c*, 1957*f*, 1964*b*, 1973*b*, 1973*c*, 1974*c*, 1975*b*, 1975*d*, 1976*d*, 1977*c*, 1979*d*, 1987*e*, 'How did Morality Get a Bad Name?', and 'Satanism and Nihilism'.

1992*e*. 'Moral Terms', 'Prescriptivism', 'Slavery', 'Universalizability', and 'Weakness of Will', in L. Becker, ed., *Encyclopedia of Ethics* (New York: Garland).

1992*f*. 'Utilitarianism and Moral Education: Comment on S. Levy's Paper', *Studies in Philosophy and Education* 11.

1993*a* 'Could Kant have been a Utilitarian?', *Utilitas* 5. Also in R. M. Dancy, ed., *Kant and Critique* (Dordrecht: Kluwer, 1993). Repr. in 1998*c*.

1993b. 'The Ethics of Medical Involvement in Torture: Comment on R. Downie's Paper', *Journal of Medical Ethics* 19.

1993c. *Essays on Bioethics* (Oxford: Oxford University Press). Contains 1974b, 1975c, 1977a, 1978a, 1983a, 1985c, 1986d, 1987d, 1987g, 1988a, 1988b, 1988d, English version of 1989e, 'Moral Problems about the Control of Behaviour', and 'Why I am only a Demi-Vegetarian'.

1993d. Guest Editorial, 'Is Medical Ethics Lost?', and letter, *Journal of Medical Ethics* 19.

1993e. 'Utilitarianism and Deontological Principles', in R. Gillon, ed., *Principles of Health Care Ethics* (Chichester: Wiley).

1993f. 'Brandt's Methods of Ethics', in B. Hooker, ed., *Rationality, Rules and Utility: New Essays on Richard Brandt's Moral Philosophy* (Boulder, Colo.: Westview).

1993g. 'Objective Prescriptions', in E. Villanueva, ed., *Naturalism and Normativity: Philosophical Issues* 4 (Atascadero, Calif.: Ridgeview). Also in A. P. Griffiths, ed., *Ethics* (Royal Institute of Philosophy Lectures 1992/3) (Cambridge: Cambridge University Press, 1993).

Objectivity is distinct from factuality. Prescriptions are objective, if all rational thinkers would agree to them. Attempts, whether intuitionistic or naturalistic, to attain moral objectivity via facts and truth conditions collapse into relativism, because these vary with cultures, whether the facts invoked are clear and empirical, or appeal to elusive notions like needs or human flourishing. Objectivity can be achieved, as Kant saw, only by following the culturally invariant logic of the moral concepts, and seeking prescriptions or maxims that rationally must be assented to. These will generate secure descriptive meanings for moral statements, and thus moral truths invariant through cultures.

1994a. 'Applied Philosophy and Moral Theory: R. M. Hare talks to *Philosophy Today*', *Philosophy Today* 38.

1994b. 'Methods of Bioethics: Some Defective Proposals', *Monash Bioethics Review* 13. Repr. in J. W. Sumner and J. Boyle, eds., *Philosophical Perspectives on Bioethics* (Toronto, Ont.: University of Toronto Press, 1996).

The right kind of eclecticism in moral philosophy consists in picking out the good points in all theories and discarding the bad, provided that this leaves one with a consistent theory. Four defective theories are considered: situation ethics, caring ethics, virtue ethics and rights-based ethics, and it is shown how to frame a theory which combines their virtues but avoids their defects.

1994c. 'Philosophie et Conflit', *Revue de Metaphysique et Morale* 99. English version in 1997b.

1994d. 'The Structure of Ethics and Morals', in P. Singer, ed., *Ethics* (Oxford: Oxford University Press).

1995*a*. Replies to Birnbacher, Corradini, Fehige, Hinsch, Hoche, Kusser, Kutschera, Lampe, Leist, Lenzen, Lumer, Millgram, Morscher, Nida-Rumelin, Rohs, Schaber, Schöne-Seifert, Spitzley, Stranzinger, Trapp, Vogler, Wimmer, and Wolf, in C. Fehige and G. Meggle, eds., *Zum moralischen Denken* (Frankfurt a. M.: Suhrkamp). Contains also German translations of 1991*a*, 1992*c*, and 1993*a*.

1995*b*. 'Off on the Wrong Foot', in J. Couture and K. Nielsen, eds., *On the Relevance of Metaethics: New Essays on Metaethics, Canadian Journal of Philosophy* Supp. 21; a reply to P. R. Foot, 'Does Moral Subjectivism Rest on a Mistake?', *Oxford Journal of Legal Studies* 15 (1995).

Foot shows her misunderstanding of myself and the issues by calling me a subjectivist and a non-cognitivist. A non-descriptivist like me can give a clear sense to 'true' and 'know' as applied to moral statements, but their truth-conditions may vary with cultures; so descriptivism, unlike my Kantian prescriptivism, cannot yield objectivity (H 1991*a*, 1993*g*). Foot's way, following Geach and Anscombe, of explaining the action-guidingness of moral judgements, via 'specific goods' is flawed, as is her account of amoralism.

1996*a*. 'Philosophy of Language in Ethics', in M. Dascal *et al.*, eds., *Handbuch Sprachphilosphie* (Berlin: De Gruyter). Repr. revised in 1998*c*.

1996*b*. 'Impératifs, prescriptions et leur logique', in M. Canto-Sperber, *Dictionnaire de philosophie morale* (Paris: Presses Universitaires de France).

Normatives and imperatives are *different* species of prescriptions. Prescriptions have to contain phrastics, tropics, neustics and clistics (H 1989*a*). Prescriptions, as illocutionary not perlocutionary acts (1.5), are subject to logic, and this makes moral reasoning possible. Claims that the logic of imperatives is different from that of indicatives are sometimes ill-founded (H 1967*d*). Probably normative logic is a form of modal logic, analogous to the usual form (*MT* 1.6); but that of imperatives is different (no square of opposition). Supervenience applies to normatives but not to imperatives. Normatives have truth-conditions, unlike imperatives, but these vary with cultures.

1996*c*. 'Foundationalism and Coherentism in Ethics', in W. Sinnott-Armstrong and M. Timmons, eds., *Moral Knowledge: New Readings in Moral Epistemology* (Oxford: Oxford University Press).

This paper attempts to mediate between the advocates of foundationalism and coherentism. Kantian foundationalism (as in the title of the *Grundlegung*) is viable; Cartesian foundationalism is not. The latter requires there to be 'foundations' which are both necessary and substantial; but there cannot be. Kantian foundationalism requires only that we adopt a logically consistent set of maxims or prescriptions; and this we can do. These have to be cotenable by our wills in the world as it is. There is a unique set of such maxims, consistent with utilitarianism, for our relations with other people.

1996d. 'A New Kind of Ethical Naturalism?', in P. French *et al.*, eds., *Moral Concepts, Midwest Studies in Philosophy* 20 (Notre Dame, Ind.: Notre Dame University Press).

There is not much new about the 'new realism'. Ethical naturalists in particular should not draw support from recent developments in metaphysics. Putnam's attempt, with his twin-earth argument, to establish a metaphysical necessity distinct from logical or conceptual and from causal necessity fails, as can be shown by arguments derived from Von Wright and Sidelle. But even if it be accepted, Horgan and Timmons (1992) have shown that Moore's open question argument can be adapted to refute the new naturalism. This move depends on a distinction similar to mine between evaluative and descriptive meaning.

1996e. 'Internalism and Externalism in Ethics', in J. Hintikka and K. Puhl, eds., *Proceedings of 18th International Wittgenstein Congress* (Vienna: Hölder-Pichler-Tempsky).

Brink's externalism is the view that one can fully endorse a moral judgement without any corresponding motivation. Brink holds that moral judgements could not be prescriptive unless they were thought to be true; but this would be like saying that (e.g.) imperatives cannot be prescriptive. The natural properties of actions, etc., are linked only contingently, not conceptually or metaphysically, to their moral properties. The link is a deliverance of our autonomous will. Brink's argument for realism from the existence of amoralism misfires. But I can support his utilitarianism by better arguments.

1996f. 'Hare: A Philosophical Self-Portrait', in T. Mautner, ed., *A Dictionary of Philosophy* (Oxford: Blackwell).

1997a. 'Preferences of Possible People', in C. Fehige and U. Wessels, eds., *Preferences* (Proceedings of Conference in Saarbrücken, 1992) (Berlin: De Gruyter).

Hajdin's view in *Dialogue* 29 (1990), excluding from moral relevance external and now-for-then preferences, is attractive. But it does not affect my argument for including as relevant the preferences of possible people. This claims that because *actual* people prefer, if happy, to exist, universalizability requires the extension of this consideration to possible people in identical situations. It supports a liberal view on abortion: if the best family planning and population policy is being followed and the number of procreated children is determinate, the non-procreation of *this* child will make room for *another* child.

1997b. 'Philosophy and Conflict', in O. Neumaier *et al.*, eds., *Applied Ethics in a Troubled World* (Proceedings of aborted 15th International Wittgenstein Congress) (Dordrecht: Kluwer). The English version of 1994c.

1997c. *Sorting Out Ethics*, containing 'A Taxonomy of Ethical Theories' (the Axel Hägerström Lectures given in Uppsala in 1991), 'Defence of the Enterprise', 1993a, 1996a, and bibliography of R. M. Hare's writings 1949–98 (Oxford: Oxford University Press).

1998a. 'Prescriptivism', in E. Craig, ed., *Routledge Encyclopedia of Philosophy* (London: Routledge).

Prescriptivism holds that moral judgements contain an element of meaning which serves to prescribe or direct actions. The history of prescriptivism includes Socrates, Aristotle, Hume, and Mill, and it has been influential also in recent times. Moral judgements also contain a factual or descriptive element, which differs between persons and cultures; but the prescriptive element remains constant. Prescriptivism can allow for moral disagreement and explain moral weakness. It can also explain better than other theories the rationality and objectivity of moral thinking.

1998b. 'A Utilitarian Approach to Ethics', in H. Kuhse and P. Singer, eds., *A Companion to Bioethics* (Oxford: Blackwell).

1998c. 'Towards Objectivity in Morals', in Ouyang Kang and S. Fuller, eds., *Contemporary British and American Philosophy and Philosophers* (Beijing: People's Press). Based on 1994d, with additional autobiographical material. In Chinese; English version planned.

1998d. Interview, 'Die Vernunft kommt zuerst', in Borchers *et al.*, eds., *Einladen zum Denken* (Vienna: Hölder–Pichler–Tempsky).

2. *Other Writings*

References in the text of the form 'Alston, W. P. (1964: 100)' are to this part of the bibliography, the last number being the page, unless otherwise indicated. Abbreviated titles of works in brackets, as used in text.

ALEXY, R. (1979). 'R. M. Hares Regeln des moralischen Argumentierens und L. Nelsons Abwegungsgesetz', in P. Schröder, ed., *Vernunft, Erkenntnis, Sittlichkeit* (Hamburg: Meiner, 1979).

ALSTON, W. P. (1964). *Philosophy of Language* (Englewood Cliffs, NJ: Prentice-Hall).

ARISTOTLE. *Prior Analytics* (*An. Pr.*), *De Interpretatione* (*De Int.*), *Metaphysics* (*Met.*), *Nicomachean Ethics* (*Eth. Nic.*). References are to Bekker pages.

AUSTIN J. L. (1961). *Philosophical Papers* (Oxford: Oxford University Press).

—— (1962). *How to Do Things with Words* (Oxford: Oxford University Press).

AUXTER, T. (1982). *Kant's Moral Teleology* (Macon, Ga.: Mercer University Press).

AYER, A. J. (1936). *Language, Truth and Logic* (London: Gollancz).

BLACKBURN, S (1984). *Spreading the Word* (Oxford: Oxford University Press).

CARNAP, R (1932). 'Überwindung der Metaphysik durch logische Analyse der Sprache', *Erkenntnis* 2.

—— (1935). *Philosophy and Logical Syntax* (London: Routledge).

—— (1942). *Introduction to Semantics* (Cambridge, Mass.: Harvard University Press).

CARROLL, Lewis (C. L. Dodgson) (1872). *Through the Looking Glass* (London: Macmillan). Cited from Nonesuch edn. (London, 1939).

CASTAÑEDA, H. (1974). *The Structure of Morality* (Springfield, Mass.: Thomas).

CHOMSKY, N. (1965). *Aspects of the Theory of Syntax* (Cambridge, Mass.: MIT Press).

CUMMISKEY, D. (1990). 'Kantian Consequentialism', *Ethics* 100.

DRYDEN, J. (1637). *The Hind and the Panther*.

EWING, A. C. (1959). *Second Thoughts in Moral Philosophy* (London: Routledge).

GIBBARD, A. (1990). *Wise Choices, Apt Feelings* (Oxford: Oxford University Press).

HÄGERSTRÖM, A. (1911). *Om moraliska förestallningars sanning* (*On the Truth of Moral Propositions*) (Inaugural Lecture, University of Uppsala). Translated with other writings by R. T. Sandin in Hägerström, *Philosophy and Religion* (Allen & Unwin, 1964).

HARE, J. E. (1996). *The Moral Gap* (Oxford: Oxford University Press).

—— and JOYNT, C. (1982). *Ethics and International Affairs* (New York: St. Martin's Press).

HARMAN, G. (1977). *The Nature of Morality* (New York: Oxford University Press).

HARRIS, N. G. E. (1992). 'Kantian Duties and Immoral Agents', *Kant-Studien* 83.

HARRISON, J. (1985). 'Utilitarianism, Universalization, Heteronomy and Necessity *or* Unkantian Ethics', in N. Potter and M. Timmons, eds., *Morality and Universality* (Dordrecht: Reidel).

HARSANYI, J. C. (1988). 'Problems with Act-Utilitarianism and with Malevolent Preferences', in Seanor and Fotion (1988).

HEMPEL, C. G. (1965). *Aspects of Scientific Explanation* (New York: Free Press).

HORGAN, T. and TIMMONS, M. (1992). 'Troubles for New Wave Moral Semantics: The Open Question Argument Revived', *Philosophical Papers* 21.

HUME, D. (1739). *A Treatise of Human Nature* (London: Noon).

KANT, I. References are to pages of earliest editions and the Royal Prussian Academy edition.

—— (1781). *Kritik der reinen Vernunft* (*KrV*) (Riga: Hartknoch). Translation by N. K. Smith, *Immanuel Kant's Critique of Pure Reason* (London: Macmillan, 1933).

KANT, I. (1785). *Grundlegung zur Metaphysik der Sitten (Gr)* (Riga: Hartknoch). Translation by H. J. Paton, *The Moral Law* (London: Hutchinson, 1948). References are to this work unless indicated.

—— (1788). *Kritik der praktischen Vernunft (KpV)* (Riga: Hartknoch). Translation by L. W. Beck, *Critique of Practical Reason* (Indianapolis, Ind.: Bobbs-Merrill, 1956).

—— (1790). *Kritik der Urteilskraft*, pt. 1 (*KU*) (Berlin: Lagarde). Translation by J. C. Meredith, *Kant's Critique of Aesthetic Judgement* (Oxford: Oxford University Press, 1911).

—— (1797). *Metaphysische Anfangsgründe der Rechtslehre (Rl)* (Königsberg: Nicolovius). Translation by J. Ladd, *The Metaphysical Elements of Justice* (Indianapolis, Ind.: Bobbs-Merrill, 1965).

—— (1797). *Metaphysische Anfangsgründe der Tugendlehre (Tgl)* (Königsberg: Nicolovius). Translation by M. Gregor, *The Doctrine of Virtue* (New York: Harper & Row, 1964).

LEWIS, D. K. (1973). *Counterfactuals* (Cambridge: Cambridge University Press).

LEWIS, H. A. and WOODFIELD, A. (1985). 'Content and Community', *Proceedings of the Aristotelian Society* supp. vol. 59.

LO, P.-C. (1981). 'A Critical Reevaluation of the Alleged "Empty Formalism" of Kantian Ethics', *Ethics* 91.

LYONS, D. (1965). *Forms and Limits of Utilitarianism* (Oxford: Oxford University Press).

MACINTYRE, A. (1984), 'Relativism, Power and Philosophy', *Proceedings of the American Philosophical Association* 59 (1985).

MACKIE, J. L. (1977). *Ethics: Inventing Right and Wrong* (Harmondsworth: Penguin).

—— (1984). 'Rights, Utility and Universalization', with reply by Hare, in R. Frey, ed., *Utility and Rights* (Minneapolis, Minn.: University of Minnesota Press).

MILL, J. S. (1843). *A System of Logic* (London: Parker).

—— (1861). *Utilitarianism, Fraser's Magazine*. Reprinted London 1863.

MILLGRAM, E. (1995). 'Inhaltsreiche ethische Begriffe und die Unterscheidung zwischen Tatsachen und Werte', in C. Fehige and G. Meggle, eds., *Zum moralischen Denken* vol. i (Frankfurt a. M.: Suhrkamp).

MOORE, G . E. (1903). *Principia Ethica* (Cambridge: Cambridge University Press).

—— (1912). *Ethics* (London: Oxford University Press).

MORRIS, C. W. (1938). 'Foundations of the Theory of Signs', *International Encyclopedia of Unified Science* i. 2 (Chicago, Ill.: Chicago University Press).

—— (1946). *Signs, Language and Behavior* (New York: Prentice-Hall).

PARFIT, D. (1984). *Reasons and Persons* (Oxford: Oxford University Press).

PIGDEN, C. (1991). 'Naturalism', in P. Singer, ed., *A Companion to Ethics* (Oxford: Blackwell).

PIPER, A. M. S. (1982). 'A Distinction without a Difference', *Midwest Studies in Philosophy* 7.

PIUS XII, POPE (1957). Allocution, *Acta Apostolicae Sedis* xxxxix. 1027–33.

PLATO. *Republic, Statesman*. References are to Stephanus pages.

PRICHARD, H. A. (1912). 'Does Moral Philosophy Rest on a Mistake?', *Mind* 21. Repr. in his *Moral Obligation* (Oxford: Oxford University Press, 1949).

PRIOR, A. N. (1955). *Formal Logic* (Oxford: Oxford University Press).

RAWLS, J. (1971). *A Theory of Justice* (Cambridge, Mass.: Harvard University Press).

RICHARDS, D. A. J. (1988). 'Prescriptivism, Constructivism and Rights', in Seanor and Fotion (1988).

ROSS, A. (1968). *Directives and Norms* (London: Routledge).

ROSS, W. D. (1930). *The Right and the Good* (Oxford: Oxford University Press).

SAUSSURE, F. DE (1916). *Cours de linguistique générale* (Paris: Payot, 1916). Translation by Wade Baskin, *Course in General Linguistics* (New York: Philosophical Press, 1959).

SEANOR, D. and FOTION, N., eds. (1988). *Hare and Critics* (Oxford: Oxford University Press).

SEARLE, J. (1969). *Speech Acts* (Cambridge: Cambridge University Press).

—— and VANDERVEKEN, D. (1985). *Foundations of Illocutionary Logic* (Cambridge: Cambridge University Press).

SIDELLE, A. (1989). *Necessity, Essence and Individuation* (Ithaca, NY: Cornell University Press).

SINGER, P. (1981). *The Expanding Circle* (New York: Farrer, Straus, Giroux).

STEVENSON, C. L. (1942), 'Moore's Arguments against Certain Forms of Ethical Naturalism', in P. Schilpp, ed., *The Philosophy of G. E. Moore* (Evanston, Ill.: Northwestern University Press).

—— (1945). *Ethics and Language* (New Haven, Conn.: Yale University Press).

STRAWSON, P. F. (1949). 'Truth', *Analysis* 9.

—— (1950). 'Truth', *Proceedings of the Aristotelian Society*, supp. vol. 24.

—— (1959). *Individuals* (London: Methuen).

TOULMIN, S. E. (1950). *An Examination of the Place of Reason in Ethics* (Cambridge: Cambridge University Press).

URMSON, J. O. (1968). *The Emotive Theory of Ethics* (London: Hutchinson. Paperback, New York: Oxford University Press, 1969).

VON WRIGHT, G. H. (1941). *The Logical Problem of Induction*, Acta Philosophica Fennica 3 (Helsinki: Soc. Philosophica).

—— (1963). *Norm and Action* (London: Routledge).

WILLIAMS, B. A. O. (1985). *Ethics and the Limits of Philosophy* (London: Fontana/Collins).

—— (1988). 'The Structure of Hare's Theory', in Seanor and Fotion (1988).

WITTGENSTEIN, L. (1953). *Philosophical Investigations* (Oxford: Blackwell).

WRIGHT, C. (1992). *Truth and Objectivity* (Cambridge, Mass.: Harvard University Press).

INDEX